BREAKING
& MENDING
DIVORCE AND GOD'S GRACE

BREAKING & MENDING

DIVORCE AND GOD'S GRACE

MARY LOU REDDING

UPPER ROOM BOOKS
NASHVILLE

Scripture quotations contained herein, unless otherwise designated, are from the New Revised Standard Version Bible, copyright © 1989 by the Division of Christian Education of the National Council of the Churches of Christ in the U.S.A. Used by permission. All rights reserved.

Scripture quotations identified KJV are from The King James Version of the Bible.

Scripture quotations identified as NJKV are from The New King James Version. Copyright © 1979, 1980, 1982, Thomas Nelson Inc., Publishers. Used by permission.

Scripture quotations designated TEV are from the *Good News Bible*, The Bible in Today's English Version. Second Edition © 1992 American Bible Society. Used by permission.

Scripture quotations designated AP are author's paraphrase.

"The Top 10 Biblical Ways to Acquire a Wife" is reprinted from *Sunstone Magazine*, September 1996, by permission.

The poem "Clean White Boxes" by the author first appeared in the May/June 1982 issue of *alive now!*, a publication of The Upper Room.

Cover Design: Meg McWhinney
Interior Design and Layout: Nancy J. Cole
First Printing 1998

The Upper Room Web Site: http://www.upperroom.org

The Library of Congress Cataloging-in-Publication Data

Redding, Mary Lou, 1950–
    Breaking and mending: divorce and God's grace / by Mary Lou Redding.
       p. cm.
    Includes biblographical references.
      ISBN 0-8358-0855-6
      1. Divorced people—Religious life. 2. Divorce—Biblical teaching. 3. Divorce—Religious aspects—Christianity. 4. Redding, Mary Lou, 1950– . I. Title.
BV4596.D58R43 1998
248.8'46—dc21   98-11786
                                                  CIP

Printed in the United States of America

For
Casey, David, Jennifer, Jennith, Judy, Lee, Robert, Sandy, Willie
and all the single adults who have been for me
a community of love, forgiveness, and healing

CONTENTS

FOREWORD

This book speaks with a compassionate voice to those who have experienced loss. Its message is tender and not harsh. The raw wound of grief is laid bare and the hope of being reconstituted is made clear. In *Breaking and Mending* the focus is on the pain that comes from divorce, but the lessons of this book can be applied to the grief work that comes from many of life's broken relationships.

With uncommon insight, Mary Lou Redding shares what can happen when two people are not wired up the same way. She shows how it can lead to the death of a dream. Her experience with divorce causes her to say, "Divorce always represents the death of a dream. In fact, it marks the death of many dreams. My divorce meant the death of God's dream for our marriage, our dreams for ourselves and for our children, our parents' and other family members' dreams." With a determined pathos the images of this book move beyond death toward wholeness.

Rare honesty surfaces on every page. The author is candid about her marriage journey and about how she came to the place where she could be honest with her husband. She is open about how she had to cope with the power of denial and the strength of public opinion. She does not dodge the hard questions like what you learn about yourself while going through divorce and while living as a single person.

This book is not about being stone-wall strong and self-sufficient. It is about where Mary Lou went for help—pastors, counselors, friends, group sessions, biblical study, prayer, and her day-to-day relationship with God. Except for a few experiences with misdirected counseling, most of these resources were a means of grace.

The author makes plain the fact that the time which follows divorce is like a cascading fear. There is a change of status, depression, loss of identity, economic uncertainties, and the danger of unhealthy relationships. She gives her straight-forward opinion about sexual conduct, dating, and handling unmet needs. These convictions are rooted in a strong, moral, and ethical standard.

Mary Lou Redding writes with clarity and conviction about how the divorce eventually lost its controlling power. Eventually her pain was healed by the strength of grace. She received grace from others but most of all she came to the place where she could accept the unconditional love of

God. She was fortunate. Not everyone traveling through the complexity of divorce sees the wisdom of turning toward grace-filled friends, a graceful congregation, and most of all a God whose other name is love. The more she could accept the unconditional love of others and of God, the more she could accept herself.

Another towering strength of this book is that it reflects upon the tangled web of divorce and its aftermath from the vantage point of biblical images and narratives. Every chapter is supported by the experiences of real people in the biblical record. Their experiences with God and with life informed the journey of Mary Lou Redding. In a word, she drew upon their spiritual resources to resource her profound need. In so doing, she places hope at the center of the stage. Thus, grace and hope become the dominant theological themes of the entire book.

Breaking and Mending will provide a wonderful resource for the church. Clergy can give copies to those who are traumatized by the loss which comes from divorce. Divorce adjustment groups will find it helpful. Congregational sensitivity will be raised, and people who are not divorced will be educated by this work.

Without blinking, Mary Lou Redding tells the reader that there is hard grief work associated with divorce, but she also shares how the grief is redeemed by grace and hope.

— Bishop Joe E. Pennel, Jr.

CHAPTER 1

BROKEN DREAMS, BROKEN PROMISES, BROKEN HEARTS

I stood looking down at my grave, my friend Susie at my side. Blades of grass a few inches high were scattered over the slightly mounded, packed brown earth. In one of those curious, dual realities that dreams offer, I was dead and buried, and alive and talking to Susie at the same time.

"But I want that apron. We'll just have to dig up the body," I said.

"Think about what you're saying," Susie said. "You've been dead four months already. By now the corpse is decomposing."

"I know, but I want that apron."

"It will be covered with maggots. The body will be rotting and repulsive. Are you sure you want the apron that badly? Is it worth it?

"Well, maybe you're right," I sighed. "Maybe it isn't worth it. Maybe I should just leave it buried." And we turned and walked away from the grave, me crying and Susie with her arm around my shoulder.

I woke with a start, knowing immediately what my dream meant: I needed to acknowledge and grieve the death of a dream, a death that I didn't want to face. My cherished dream for my life was represented by the white organza apron in which I had been buried—a heavily starched, circular one with a ruffle, tied in a large bow behind my back. The apron was a symbol of a shirtwaist-and-pearls, perfect-homemaker image I carried in my mind. That apron represented something important to me: my desire to have a home and family. I even referred to my "Susie Homemaker" life, using the name of a line of toys (miniature kitchen appliances) that were popular when I was growing up. As is often the case with dreams, my friend Susie was there as part of an obvious pun on the name I had given my dream. Her comforting presence also encouraged me to admit something I had not been willing to face in my waking hours: my dream was dead.

But I was struggling with that. For years before I married, I had prayed for the man who would one day be my husband. I had dreamed of marrying a good Christian man, of caring for a home and children. In fact, after I married, if I was interrupted by a telephone call while cleaning or cooking and the caller asked what I was doing, I'd often say, "Oh, I'm just being Susie Homemaker." That phrase gathered up a set of images and desires that I had carried in my heart for many years. But now I was divorced. Me, a Christian married to a Christian, divorced. How could this have happened?

We had promised to love each other until death. Instead we had hurt each other time after time, year after year. We had failed each other; I had failed myself, and I felt I had failed God. I knew that God was grieving too, and that was almost more than I could bear. I had never planned to be here; I didn't want to be here, and I was having trouble letting go of the dream, even though my marriage was legally over.

In trying to make sense of this struggle, I did what I always do: I looked to the Bible. In its stories I always find guidance, and as I reflected on my marriage, the story of Hosea and Gomer helped me to look at my situation. The prophet Hosea surely knew about the pain of a troubled marriage. After several years, his wife Gomer left him and their three children. They were separated for some time, with Gomer becoming a prostitute.

Hosea's actions toward Gomer show him to be a loving and forgiving man, a person of faith. He must have been wounded and confused by the situation in which he found himself. The opening verses of the Book of Hosea tell us that Hosea felt God had told him to marry this woman. Here was a man who was talking with God and listening to God about his relationships. I feel sure that he married with the same dreams in his heart as any bridegroom has, dreams of having a home and family. He probably wasn't all that different than many of us. I can imagine his excitement when their first son was born. The boy was given the name Jezreel, which means "God sows," a hopeful name that both acknowledges the child as a gift from God and looks forward to what God will bring to fruit. But by the time their second child, a daughter, was born, things seem to have changed. Hosea gives this child the name Lo-ruhamah, which means "Not pitied" or "Not loved." The third child, another son, was given the name Lo-ammi, which means "Not my people."

As with all the prophets, we have to recognize that this story is meant to make a point about God's dealings with Israel. Many modern scholars say that Gomer and the children in this story are metaphors, literary devices and not real people at all. But the story is told to illustrate deep love and deep pain; Hosea told it to help his hearers receive a message by entering into the story. And like every good story, it invites us to consider many levels of meaning. It is a picture of love and how we can wound and be wounded in relationships. What else but love could cause a husband to stand by such a wife when she humiliated him and their children? What else but love could make him go out and buy her back from whatever brothel owner was using her? But surely that was not what Hosea had wanted for their life together. He knew about the pain of shattered dreams. He knew firsthand about broken promises and broken hearts.

The story of Hosea and Gomer helps me to consider that even God's people often find themselves entangled in painful and damaging relationships. Praying about our relationships and trying to listen to God do not guarantee that we will make right decisions and live happily ever after.

Part of the difficulty, of course, is that we do not always hear God clearly. I have difficulty believing God would tell someone to marry an adulterous person. Hosea understood God to be telling him to marry an adulterous person, but that's only one way to look at the situation and at what God said. As I think about God's direction to Hosea, I replay in my head the way my mother sometimes spoke to me. When I had made up my mind to do something, Mother would often in exasperation say something like, "Fine, then. You do whatever you think." She could see when I had made up my mind; she knew me well enough to see when it was useless to try to stop me. Maybe Hosea had gone to God with his plan to marry Gomer, asking God's blessing, and God had tried to dissuade him. Maybe what Hosea heard as "Go and marry an adulterous woman" was God saying, "I've tried to get you to see that this is a bad idea, but I won't stop you. I can see you've made up your mind. Go on and do it, then, and see what happens. And I will use even this to teach you something about my love."

And so Hosea married Gomer. But somewhere between the birth of Jezreel, "God sows," and Lo-ruhamah, "Not loved," Hosea's view of the world changed. Imagine him saying his daughter's name, knowing it meant "not loved." Perhaps the child was not loved because she was born at a time when Hosea and Gomer were too unhappy to be able to love her. Or Hosea may have given the child that name as a symbol of his own feelings because his marriage was failing and he was reminded every day that Gomer did not love him. Or perhaps he thought Gomer felt unloved. Maybe he told himself that if he had loved her more, she could have changed, she could have been happy with him and their family. Living with "Not loved" must have been very painful, being reminded daily that the love was gone.

From my own experience, I know that it can be. During the second year of our marriage, my husband Spencer came to me one Saturday morning and said, "I need to talk to you. Something is bothering me, and I need to get it off my chest." We sat down on the sofa and he said, "I need to tell you something. This has been on my mind for a long time, and I just have to say it: I don't love you. I didn't love you when I married you, and I'm not sure I'll ever be able to love you."

Stunned, I could only stare at him. This was the romantic man who sent me flowers, who brought me gifts. How could he be saying this? I felt as if my throat was closing, as if I'd been kicked in the stomach. I couldn't breathe. My stomach knotted up. Finally I managed to recover my voice enough to whisper, "If you didn't love me, why did you marry me?"

"Because you're the kind of woman I want to be the mother of my children."

I didn't know what to do. What is your next step when your husband says something like that? Finally I went to the phone and called our pastor. We met with him the next afternoon, and my husband and I started down a long road of counseling, trying to save our marriage.

But after that day, it was as if "Not loved" lived with us. Many times every day I was reminded that I was not loved. Without even realizing it, Spencer would send daggers through me with a word or gesture that reminded me of some past act of tenderness. It had all been a lie—the wedding vows, the cards, the love letters—all of it. I was not loved. The wedding pictures on the wall reminded me of it; wearing the cameo he had given me for my birthday reminded me of it; his taking my hand as we walked into church reminded me of it. I had believed that if we were both Christians, with God's help there was no problem that we could not overcome. But how can a home be built without love? I was not loved, and day after day, the pain of knowing that stuck in my throat. I could not get past it. I cried for myself and for my husband.

After a few sessions of talking with our pastor, Spencer decided that he did not need to go any more. He was fine, he told me. Though he wasn't happy with me, he did not believe in divorce and felt we could continue as we were. When the pastor suggested that I talk with a counselor alone, I did, working through the immediate hurt of this situation and also dealing with old hurts that I had never confronted. It was as if facing this new pain opened the door to other pain I had buried inside for years. Months passed, and Spencer and I settled into a routine. We did not talk about the gulf between us. I continued in counseling, trying to understand my husband's feelings and my own. One of the things I realized was that keeping the wedding vows I had made before God was very important to me, even more important than whether I was happy. I believed we had married for life, and even if Spencer did not love me, I loved him. To be a person of integrity, I had to stay. Like Hosea, I was unwilling to give up on my marriage.

Hosea continued to love Gomer. The Bible tells us that he went out and bought her back, out of prostitution, out of bondage, and brought her home. It may sound like a wonderful love story, but there were harsh realities as well. Hosea had to face the stares and whispers of his neighbors. The children had to cope with what their mother had done. And think about Gomer. Imagine what she must have endured while working as a prostitute. Prostitutes often endure abuse of various kinds, and she had probably experienced all kinds of degradation. When Hosea brought her home, along with them came all the wounds Gomer had suffered during her time away and all the wounds he had suffered in being left.

Even though Hosea brought her back, this was no idyllic reconciliation, all their problems solved by their love. The Bible tells us that Hosea said to her, "You must remain as mine . . . you shall not have intercourse with a man, nor I with you" (Hos. 3:3). This can be read many ways. Perhaps Hosea knew about venereal disease and wanted to protect himself; perhaps he knew somehow that the love Gomer most needed had to be nonsexual; perhaps he considered her unclean and believed sexual contact with her would make him continually unclean. Whatever the reasons, their relationship could never be what it had been before. Though they were married, it was not a storybook marriage. Though Hosea loved her, he faced the reality of what their relationship could and could not be. It must have been a painful reality.

Sometimes it is difficult to remember that along with their strengths, persons bring into relationships all their wounds. When I married Spencer, I married everything that he was. He was handsome and funny and romantic, and we had much in common. We both loved music and art and books and ideas; we loved shopping for antiques together. We loved bridge and often played far into the night with our best friends. We attended church together and were heavily involved in our Sunday school class and in a small growth group. But Spencer also brought his wounds, just as I brought mine—including the ones I had never dealt with.

As I continued seeing the counselor, I began telling my husband about things I had never told anyone, acknowledging my pain and weaknesses, allowing him to know me more deeply than I had ever allowed anyone to know me. I tried to be totally honest with him about my feelings and my struggles, consciously allowing myself to be vulnerable with him, thinking that doing so would forge a bond between us. It was a great risk. But I was becoming freer and freer. I was able to look squarely at my painful past and acknowledge it without being immobilized by the pain. As I began feeling better about myself, I was changing. That meant my relationship with Spence had to change too. But he did not want it to change. He had told me he was content with things as they were, and he meant it. We began arguing, and one day he lashed out at me, throwing up to me things from my past, painful experiences I had told him in moments of vulnerability. I did not understand how he could use my confidences to taunt me.

Like me, he carried inner pain, needs, and insecurities. It is painful to realize that sometimes people cannot be what we need or want them to be, just as we cannot be what they need or want us to be. As much as Hosea loved Gomer, she could not be the pure and faithful wife he wanted her to be. As much as she might have loved him, she could not be other than what she was. As much as I cared for Spencer, he and I could not be what the other needed. And not only were we not what the other needed; we were hurting one another in many ways.

In the middle of a night near the end of my marriage, I woke as I often did, feeling an enormous sadness like a heavy weight on my chest. I knew from experience that I would not be going back to sleep, so I slipped out of bed in order not to wake Spencer and went to lie on the sofa. I hugged a pillow to muffle my sobs, asking God to help me. Though I cared for my husband, by simply being the person I was, I caused him pain. And without him realizing it or meaning to, he was hurting me over and over again. We were locked in a dance that felt like death.

I felt as if I were disappearing, as if the person I was, was being used up. After years of pouring all my emotional energy into this relationship, I finally had to admit to myself that I felt like I was dying inside. I could not go on. It was a terrible realization. I could not make it better; Spencer could not make it better. It was not a matter of killing our marriage. The relationship was really already dead. I had to face the reality of our limits as people. I didn't want to face it, but I could not make this marriage work.

I know that people stay in marriages where day after day, in countless ways, they are shown and even told as I was that they are not loved, that they do not matter. Spouses make choices that say they do not cherish their mates. People become addicted to work or money or relationships or power, and their husbands or wives mourn. When we are not loved, we often come to feel that we are not lovable. And eventually, the physical or emotional or spiritual pain catches up with us, and we have to acknowledge that we cannot go on.

Why was it so difficult for me to do that? Why did I struggle so? It was a combination of self-righteousness, pride, and my wrong understanding of how God deals with us. I had always tried as hard as I could to be a good Christian. I wanted more than anything to be a person whose life and beliefs match. If I said I believed in marriage, in fidelity, in unconditional love, then I had to make my marriage work. Admitting that I could not was admitting a personal failing as well as a spiritual one. Good Christians don't get divorces, I thought, and I wanted to be a good Christian.

I also had to admit that I could not control my life. Though I always couched my assertions in theologically acceptable phrases, using scripture to support them, basically I believed that if we believe rightly and try to do God's will as we understand it, we can do any worthwhile thing we set out to do. "With God all things are possible," I had heard, and surely saving a marriage was the sort of thing that God would want to make possible. Still, I found myself crying late at night, in more pain than I could ever remember, wanting more than anything to love and be loved. But I could not make it happen.

I had to surrender my dream, surrendering along with it the future for which I had prayed. What could I do? Nothing. I was frightened. If I could not help myself, if I could not take care of myself, who would take care of me? What could I do but turn to God, the Faithful One? Finally, I had to give up. I had to say that all I could do was trust God, the only one who is unfailingly faithful. I had no other answers than to believe that somehow the love of God was mine and that somehow the love of God would fill in the gaps between what I wanted to do and be and what I was able to do and be. Believing that I was supposed to be perfect was a lie, one that had kept me isolated for years in my pain and one that kept me from opening myself to receive the love and comfort God offers each of us.

Far from condemning, God was hurting with us, grieving for our broken dreams and for my husband and me. God was not pleased with our behavior; God always grieves when we harm one another. But just as God loved and reached out to the people of Israel even when they willfully sinned, God continued to love me and reach out to me.

Acknowledging the pain and the loss was an important part of letting God heal me. I didn't want to hurt any more, and so I didn't want to grieve. But grieving is a part of every death, every loss. God came to me in my dream about the apron, saying to me, "It's time to face the truth: this relationship is dead. You can't make it right. Grieve for what you've lost, and then we can move on."

Divorce always represents the death of a dream. In fact, it marks the death of many dreams. My divorce meant the death of God's dream for our marriage, our dreams for ourselves and our children, our parents' and other family members' dreams. When Hosea spoke to the Israelites, he told them that their faithlessness had consequences not just for them but for the land and even the animals. As Hosea 4:1-3 says, "There is no faithfulness or loyalty. . . . Swearing, lying, and murder, and stealing and adultery break out; bloodshed follows bloodshed. Therefore the land mourns, and all who live in it languish; together with the wild animals and the birds of the air, even the fish of the sea are perishing." Our actions always have consequences for us and for our community. When a marriage ends, the effects ripple outward from the two spouses to their children, their families, their church, their neighborhood. Though the grief and loss vary in intensity, everyone around us is affected. Grandparents may grieve for or fear the loss of frequent contact with grandhcildren; in-laws may grieve loss of contact with a family member they have loved for years; cousins may grieve the loss of seeing one another at family dinners every weekend or family gatherings at holidays. So it goes, on many levels. When a marriage dies, many people grieve. I loved my family-by-marriage. I didn't want to lose them, either. A failed relationship is a tear in the fabric of community, and I could see that. I knew a divorce would cause great pain.

Even when we are trying to follow God faithfully, there are no guarantees that our lives will be what we want them to be. But I didn't want to believe that. Along with my dream, I had to surrender some of my naivete. And in doing so, I found God opening a new way before me. As I acknowledged my limits, I came to believe that God is faithful even when we cannot be. For me, it was a new understanding of grace.

CHAPTER 2

GOOD-BYE ANSWERS, HELLO QUESTIONS

So how did I get to where I found myself? If I didn't want to be divorced and didn't plan to be divorced, how did I end up divorced? The story has some twists and turns in it, and it took me a long time—years—to make the journey.

Within twenty-four hours of the time my husband told me that he did not love me, we met with our pastor. I knew we had to try to save our marriage; I just didn't know where to begin. After we talked about the events of the day before, the pastor asked us why we married, what it was about the other that originally attracted us, and what we liked about each other now. He asked each of us to make a list and bring it to our next meeting so we could see what we had to build on. This was not difficult for me. I loved Spencer—from time to time I wanted to choke him, but I figured most wives and husbands feel that way occasionally—and I was clear about the reasons I loved him. My list had over sixty items on it. Spencer's list had several items on it, so the pastor's question had helped him go beyond seeing me just as the person he wanted to have as mother of his children. We met with the pastor again to begin talking about our marriage.

Spencer soon said he didn't feel the need to continue the sessions. I was the one who had had the troubled childhood and the family problems. That was true, and I assumed that most of our difficulties stemmed from my emotional scars. When the pastor had suggested that I continue in counseling alone, I went eagerly. I wanted a good marriage, and I would do anything I could to achieve that.

I believed that our attitudes shape our lives. As Abraham Lincoln is supposed to have said, "Most people are about as happy as they make up their minds to be."

I had decided long before my marriage to be happy and upbeat about life. The book *Pollyanna* had made a big impression on me when I was a child, and though I thought the fictional Pollyanna was a bit much, I could see that concentrating on what was good has its advantages. Dr. Norman

Vincent Peale's book *The Power of Positive Thinking* had affected our culture while I was growing up too and Napoleon Hill's *Think and Grow Rich* philosophy, "Whatever you can conceive and believe, you can achieve," had made its way into much popular psychology. Positive-thinking and sales seminars still teach that we all can become, if not millionaires, at least very successful by learning the right techniques to manipulate circumstances (and our customers). Seminars on shaping our destiny by changing our ways of thinking were springing up everywhere, and various philosophies and religions told us that by achieving inner peace and harmony we could shape the outer world to our liking. And all of this was reinforced by the often-repeated belief that in America anyone can become anything.

But adopting a positive, "winner" lifestyle went beyond pop psychology for me. I had become a Christian as a teenager, in a conservative church. My family members were not Christian and were at times vocally anti-Christian, and I felt an enormous responsibility to be a witness to them. Though they would not listen if I tried to say much about my faith, I felt that they could not ignore my life. So every part of my life, from obeying my parents to being a good student, became a part of my Christian witness. Everything about my life had to be exemplary because my witness might win my family to God.

Spencer and I had met at a Christian college, and we attended church together, prayed together, and worked in various kinds of outreach together. Before the crisis in my marriage, I had no reason to question whether I was happy. I had a Christian husband who loved me, a job I enjoyed, and a wonderful circle of supportive Christian friends. Of course I was happy. Why wouldn't I be happy?

Growing up, I had absorbed traditional beliefs about the roles of men and women. My mother was a stand-by-your-man kind of woman. Advice-column lists like "Ten Commandments for Wives" with their admonitions always to be supportive and never to criticize one's husband in public were for Mother models of right behavior. She showed great disdain for any wife who spoke ill of her husband, and when we heard of a man's infidelity, Mother would say something like, "Well, you can't steal away a man who's happy. There must be something wrong at home." Divorce was a terrible thing, especially if there were children, and couples should stay together "for the sake of the kids." Her pronouncements about marriage and relationships reflected the culture and times in which she grew up, and they played like tapes in my mind.

During college I had heard a great deal of conservative Bible teaching that caused me to adopt the attitude that in marriage the woman is responsible for the atmosphere of the home. The man is the spiritual head of the home, and a Christian wife honors and submits to her husband, regardless of what he does. This, layered onto the traditional beliefs I had absorbed from Southern culture, made it very difficult for me to acknowledge the problems in our marriage. Looking back now, I realize I was hiding from reality.

Some months after Spencer's announcement that he did not love me, he told me he had decided that he did love me after all. That was enough for me. If he loved me and we worked at it, we could make our marriage good.

As a matter of fact, in my sessions with the therapist I spent much of the time talking about my childhood and young adulthood and avoiding the issues in my marriage. But as the weeks and months passed, I came to understand the power my past had over me in the present. Before counseling, I felt as if I had been dragging an enormous bag of emotional garbage behind me everywhere I went. In counseling I was taking the garbage out, examining it, and letting go of it. The bag wasn't empty, but it was getting smaller and lighter. Freed from carrying the heavy load of old hurts, I had more emotional and physical energy. There came a time when the counselor asked me what I wanted to work on next, and I the only thing I could identify was communication issues in my marriage. The counselor suggested that Spence and I participate in a couples group. When Spence refused to attend after a few sessions, I decided to continue. I figured I could learn by hearing how other couples dealt with their challenges. I also began reading every book I could find on Christian marriage. If there were strategies out there to improve my marriage and make me a better wife, I was determined to find them.

And I prayed. I prayed for my husband, and I prayed for myself. I asked God to help Spence in every way. I asked God to help me be a more supportive, more loving, more submissive wife. I fasted. I asked God to take the sacrifice of my fasting and use it to bring a miracle in our marriage. And still I did not confide in anyone about the troubles we were having. Spencer seemed more and more unhappy, in spite of all that I did.

Soon he suggested that we change churches, and I agreed. Though I would miss the closeness of the neighborhood church we had attended, the bigger church offered Sunday school classes especially for young married couples. I thought that having these people as friends would help us. Here we heard more conservative teaching about almost everything, including marriage and the roles of husbands and wives.

I decided that our problems came from us not properly filling the roles God had ordained for us. If I could be supportive enough, Spence would feel better about himself and be happier with me. If I did not question his financial maneuverings, there would be less tension in our home. If I did everything right, my marriage would be wonderful. For the next few years, I gave myself wholeheartedly to strengthening our marriage. It was my spiritual project, the focus of my emotional energy.

I told no one about the terrible insecurity I felt or about Spencer's endless criticisms of me. I wasn't thin enough or a good enough hostess or an enthusiastic enough lover. I was deeply ashamed that I could not do better. If I could just whip myself into shape, our life would be fine. In the meantime, I pretended to the world that all was well.

But all was not well. I poured more and more of my energy into our marriage. I had nothing left over to give to my job, to the church, even to my relationship with God. How could I reach out to others to share the love of God when I was struggling day by day to survive emotionally? All my praying and maneuvering were not working, not at all. Neither of us was getting our deep needs met, but I could not tell anyone about our struggles. Doing so would be disloyal.

My lifeline during this time was Al, my counselor. Week after week, he welcomed me as I was. I couldn't fathom why. I was failing my husband, myself, and God, and I didn't deserve acceptance. My understanding of grace was not pardon but parole. I was a prisoner temporarily released—convicted and vulnerable to being rearrested if I did anything wrong. If I toed the mark, if I was carefully and consistently good, I was forgiven. But if I were to do something wrong, all the original charges against me would be immediately reinstated. In this understanding of grace, our good standing with God is a fragile thing. Hitting the slightest bump in our moral road causes God to un-forgive us. I could not conceive of a God who could love me in spite of all my flaws and weaknesses. But I slowly grew to trust Al and to believe that he cared about me as I was. I was able to tell him my deepest secrets, to talk about the most reprehensible parts of myself. To my amazement, he did not recoil from me. On the contrary, he received me lovingly and encouraged me to talk about my hurts, my fears, my sins and struggles.

As weeks and months passed, Al kept reminding me that I was worth loving, even with my flaws, and that we do not have to earn God's love and forgiveness. I didn't believe him. But one day as I sat in his office, struggling to understand this, I realized that he knew more bad things about me than anyone ever had—and I could feel that he also loved and valued me and wanted only the best for me. As I sat clutching the cushion of that familiar vinyl chair, my spiritual eyes were suddenly opened. I know of no other way to say it than that. I suddenly understood that if Al could do this, maybe God could. Until that moment, I had not grasped the truth that God loves us unconditionally, not for our potential but for who we are, for our inherent worth. I had read about it and talked about it, but I had never grasped it on a personal level. It was only as I experienced unconditional love from another human being that I could glimpse the possibility of that kind of love and a much greater love from God.

It was a completely different way of looking at myself and at others. In my world growing up, parents loved kids who behaved, kept their rooms clean, and did as they were told: teachers loved kids who did their homework and obeyed the rules; the church approved of those who read the Bible, prayed, and tithed. Al showed me that there is another way to love people. I read something Paul Tournier had written about an experience that was "a juicy taste of the grace of God," and immediately I realized that was what Al's friendship was for me. I had glimpsed a truth that changed the way I saw God, myself, and the world.

All along the way during my counseling, Spencer and I talked openly about the things I was dealing with, and though he did not understand why the past could cause pain in the present, he accepted that that was so. I felt free and happier than I ever had. But I was also different than I had been. I was learning not to bury my feelings, and Spencer found that troublesome. When I was unhappy, I cried. When I was angry, I said so. Emotions are often inconvenient and untidy, and he did not like having them out in the open. He had been reared always to be nice, and anger and tears just did not fit into his conception of what a nice Christian family ought to be. I was living by a different script than he wanted us to live by, and that did not make him happy. More and more, his unhappiness became obvious, and I asked him once again to see a counselor with me. We went to a few sessions, and he told me that he didn't need this. If I needed it, that was fine and I should continue, but he would not.

I examined my feelings and needs and prayed for help, trying day by day to give Spencer the unconditional love that I had discovered, believing that was what he most needed from me. I had reached a plateau in my counseling sessions, so I stopped going regularly. I felt good about honoring my commitment to my husband and my wedding vows.

I was working full time and attending graduate school, and we were part of a close-knit community of Christians who had gone to the same college. In addition to our church commitments, we lived near each other and engaged in ministry together. I also began working part time on the church staff, editing the church newspaper and doing other writing tasks. With school and work and community and church activities, we were so busy that I didn't have much time to stop and ask myself if I was happy. And besides, I didn't want to answer that question.

By this time we had been married for several years, and we decided that it was time to have a baby. Though I was never consciously aware of remembering Spence's statement about the kind of woman he wanted as mother of his children, I wonder how that played into my eagerness to have a baby. Anyway, having a child would strengthen the bond between us and show the world that all was well with us and our marriage. Eventually I became pregnant. I felt wonderful, as if I owned the world.

But alongside the wonder of being pregnant, I worried about what we would do when I had to leave work. The company I worked for gave only unpaid leaves of absence for maternity leave, and that meant we would have to depend on Spencer's earnings alone. After our daughter was born, I became more and more scared. Bills went unpaid because there was no money to pay them. I refrained from criticizing Spencer and tried not to voice my worries, believing that God would take care of us. But finally the day came when our water was disconnected because the bill had not been paid. I was sitting at home with a tiny baby, with dirty diapers to wash, and there was no water. In addition to being scared, I was angry—at God and at Spencer. Vulnerable as I was, I should not be in this situation. I had learned in counseling to identify my feelings and to be honest about them, and I knew I had to talk to someone. I decided to confide in one of the pastors at our church.

When I told him about our situation, he told me that if I would be the wife God wanted me to be, God would make Spencer the husband God wanted him to be. He urged me to pray about this and assured me he would pray for us too. I wanted to believe what he said; I had read numerous books that told of women being godly wives and finding their marriages transformed, and I wanted that to happen for us. I choked down my fear and went back home.

We got through that crisis, and after I returned to work we settled back into our old routine. Being a parent was a lot harder than I thought it would be, but every day held new discoveries as Emily's personality unfolded. She had her father's sunny disposition and was endlessly pleasant and affectionate. Our baby was a wonderful gift, and we both adored her. Was I happy? I told myself that I was.

As the months passed, however, it became clear to me that nothing was different or was likely to be in the future. I saw what I did not want to see, that I was the one willing to work on this relationship. My energy would have to sustain it. And my shortcomings continued to be the focus of our interaction. Everything about me was wrong, and according to my husband, my inadequacies were the reasons for our difficulties. I was like the character in Greek mythology who was punished by having his liver eaten away every day by birds. Each night his liver grew back, and the next day the torture would begin again. The pain was not going to stop.

Finally, I told Spencer that I was feeling scared and sad and unsure about whether I could stay in our marriage. I had been pouring myself into our relationship for years, and I was near a breaking point. I felt I was being used up. This relationship was slowly eating away at me. Day by day, the person I really was, was disappearing, and in her place was someone who was plastic, not a real person but an imitation.

This time, Spence was the one who suggested that we talk to our pastor. The pastor suggested counseling, but Spencer was still adamant that he did not need it, that I was the maladjusted and unhappy one. He was in favor of me seeing someone, however. All the other times, counseling had helped renew my resolve to stay in the marriage. Maybe it would this time too. I told Spencer clearly that if I stayed, I had to be able to do so freely and wholeheartedly. Could I stay if things were always going to be as they were then? That was the question I had to answer.

Part of the difficulty for me was the absence of what many call "scriptural grounds" for divorce. Neither of us had been unfaithful; I could not conceive of either of us ever being. Spencer was a sincere, honest, dedicated Christian. In my understanding of scripture, if we divorced I could never remarry. I would be alone, and I would be rearing our daughter alone.

So once more I began seeing a counselor, this time a wonderful, transplanted Southern Baptist with a Southern accent as thick and as charming as Spence's. Ben's manner made me feel I could make the most outrageous statement in the world and have it be met with, "That's interesting. Tell me more about that." Coming from a conservative, evangelical background, he understood my struggle about scripture, as well as many of the other cultural patterns that Spencer and I brought into our marriage.

Each week when I returned from my session, Spencer would ask, "How did it go?"

"It went fine."

"Have you made a decision yet?"

"No, not yet. When I do, I'll tell you." Sometimes he'd ask what we had talked about, and I would tell him in general that we had talked about feelings or about unmet needs or about honesty. Unfailingly civil and pleasant, Spence and I continued to eat meals together, attend church and our small group together, and talk about our common interests, though always I moved through the days with a heavy weight of pain in my chest.

The pain was immobilizing me. Day after day, I made myself get up, go to work, care for Emily, and do what I had to do. It was as if all the lightness had gone out of life. There were no good days, only some days that weren't as bad as others. But I could not bring myself to say that I wanted a divorce. Ben and I talked often about my inability to make a decision. Finally, in one session as I talked about the future, I made a statement something like, "When I have to do this by myself..." and Ben stopped me.

"Did you hear what you just said?"

"What?"

"Repeat that last statement." I did, and he said, "What does that say to you?"

"That I've made the decision but I just don't know it?"

"What do you think?" I had to admit it seemed that somewhere inside I had made the leap. On some level, I knew what the outcome would eventually be and what I would do. I drove home that day crying. As I exited the interstate, I prayed with tears rolling down my cheeks, "Dear God, I can't do this unless I am absolutely sure. This is too hard. It goes against too much of what I've been taught and believe. I have to know for sure." In answer to that prayer, God gave me a great gift of certainty. I knew that getting a divorce was the right decision for me, even though it seemed contrary to much that I understood. It wasn't what I wanted or ever would have predicted, but deep inside I knew that it was what I had to do. From that moment, I was sure. I needed to be sure because I would soon face an onslaught of advice and censure from many people I loved and respected.

But first I had to tell Spencer. I didn't do it that night. I went on to work at the church the next day, composing in my head what I would say when we talked that evening. But I never had the opportunity to make the speech. Midafternoon, my phone rang. It was Spence. I had been crying, and he could tell. He asked what was the matter, but I didn't want to tell him. Finally, he asked, "What is it? Have you decided?"

"I didn't want to tell you this way. I wanted us to be face to face. But yes, I've decided. I can't stay in this marriage." I was crying, and he was absolutely silent. Finally I said, "Can we talk about this tonight? There's a lot I need to say to you."

That night, I told him I felt strongly that this was what I had to do, that I could not go on as we were. He sat with his elbows on his knees, hands clasped, and let his head fall forward. Then he sighed. When he lifted his head to look at me, I expected to see pain in his eyes. There was pain, but even more clearly I also saw relief. I was surprised to realize that on some level he was glad it was over too.

As incredible as it may sound, we agreed that we wanted to behave like Christians during the process of getting a divorce. We agreed that when people asked questions we would not reveal details about our diffi- culties. At the end of our talk, we prayed together. Each of us asked for God's help, for ourselves and for the other. We prayed for our daughter and for wisdom in dealing with her, and we asked God to help us with what lay ahead.

When I told our small group that I was filing for divorce, they implored me to consider something less drastic. I was making a horrible mistake, they said. They pledged to help save our marriage. They prayed for us and "claimed [our] marriage for God." They suggested that we talk to the pastor. They told me they were going "to believe God for a miracle of restoration."

As strange as it sounds, their opposition was important to what I was learning. God was shaking me loose from a limited way of looking at my faith, at the world, and at grace. My formulas for dealing with life were being challenged.

Life is not linear, and faith is not linear. Gradually I was coming to understand that. There are no guarantees about anything in life, even for those who follow God with all their hearts. Think about the witness of scripture. Daniel prayed three times a day and ended up in a lion's den. Meshach, Shadrach, and Abednego were faithful to God's way and ended up in a fiery furnace. Jeremiah proclaimed God's truth faithfully and ended up at the bottom of a well. Job loved and served God and lost everything. Mary "found favor with God" and ended up unmarried, pregnant, and threatened with divorce. Paul was shipwrecked three times, flogged, and imprisoned. Jesus was perfectly obedient to God, and he was crucified. I could go on, but the bottom line is clear: sometimes life is unfair and harsh, even for those who are following God. We can do our best and still end up in a rotten situation. It was hard for me to admit this.

At the root of this, for me, was the warm and wonderful illusion (maybe delusion might be more accurate) that we can control our circumstances. In both secular and Christian arenas, we are taught that we have the power to get what we want out of life and other people. We can get what we want from our husbands and wives, we can rear compliant and untroubled children who will adopt our faith without question, we can succeed in business and always be prosperous—because after all, God wants us to have "life, and that . . . more abundantly" (John 10:10, KJV). We want to believe that we have power over what happens to us, that we can shape our circumstances. At least, I wanted to believe those things. If we do one, two, and three, four is sure to follow. Think about our love for simple solutions. The little books of maxims that are so popular right now are an example of it. Robert Fulghum's book *All I Needed to Know about Life I Learned in Kindergarten* was a phenomenal success because we want to believe that life really is that simple, that we can reduce every struggle and situation to a problem to be solved by applying a set of rules that someone else will give us. The more recent *Seven Habits of Highly Effective People* (with its sequel, *Seven Habits of Highly Effective Families*) has been a similar success among business types. When these systems wane in popularity, someone else will come along with another list (usually with ten or fewer items on it) that we will adopt. We love to believe that this—whatever the current "this" is—will take care of our struggles and make life what we want it to be.

I was no different. All of the strategies I used to try to save my marriage were attempts to make formulas work. The books I read and many of the Bible teachers I heard made it clear that their strategies were God's truth and would work if I worked them faithfully. I spent years investing myself in following these strategies.

The story of Jeremiah with the people of Israel and the false prophets is about people who are a lot like me. It's a story about people who prefer neat and easy answers over the truth. (See Jeremiah 27–29.) God's people are about to be carried into exile. Jeremiah has been sent by God to prepare them for what is ahead, to tell them that the captivity will be long and difficult. But false prophets tell the people that the exile will be short, that they will soon be back home. The people prefer to listen to the false prophets because they are saying what the people want to hear.

It is always tempting to listen to what we want to hear: God wants us to be prosperous. It's a lovely dress, and no, it doesn't make your hips look large. That's a great idea; I'll think about it and get back to you. And they lived happily ever after—"the happy ending" that Kathleen Norris says in *Dakota: A Spiritual Geography* is "the happiest lie of all."[1] These attractive lies are much easier to listen to than difficult truths. Like the Jews who didn't want to listen to Jeremiah and instead clung to what they wanted to hear, I had clung to what I wanted to hear—that I could love my husband into changing, that God would heal my marriage, that everything was going to be all right. There were plenty of good people who believed that, just as the false prophets believed what they were telling God's people about the exile. We often refuse to hear the truth and settle for some comfortable lie that will require less of us. Hard as it was to stay in my marriage, facing my mistake and getting a divorce would be even harder. For years I listened to the voices that allowed me to reinforce my denial or at least kept me from seeing that what was before me was getting worse. Jesus told the disciples that they were to be in the world but not of it. Being in the world means looking at reality. It means not living in a fantasy or searching for a fairy-tale existence.

I can understand the desire to latch on to what sounds sure. We want life to be reliable, to proceed according to the rules. My failed marriage challenged many of my assumptions about faith and about how God works in our lives. As Ecclesiastes tells us, "The race is not to the swift, nor the battle to the strong, nor bread to the wise, nor riches to the intelligent, nor favor to the skillful; but time and chance happen to them all" (Eccles. 9:11).

Life happens to us. Life is filled with things over which we have no power. We can pray, fast, wheedle, manipulate and try subtly and not so subtly to influence others, but we cannot control what life hands us. I did not want to admit this. After all, who wants to hear bad news? Most of us don't, and sometimes I think especially in the church we don't. There's a church in my neighborhood that had on its message board the saying, "Having a bad day? Just pray." The implication is that if we pray, we won't have bad days, or at least that bad days will become good ones. It's the God-the-heavenly-bellhop school of theology: Need something? Just call room service, and someone will bring it right to you. Just ask God, and it will be taken care of. No problem.

Many of the people I knew and loved applied their faith to life in ways that resembled formulas. For instance, Mark 11:23 says that we can command our physical environments, that we "shall have whatsoever" we say. That means that what we say is extremely important. If we say something negative, we risk making that negative thing happen. If we want something from God, speaking positively moves that desire closer to reality. This theology supported my friends' affirmations such as, "We are believing God for a miracle of restoration." Another example: Matthew 18:18-20 says, "If two of you shall agree on earth as touching any thing that they shall ask, it shall be done for them of my Father which is in heaven. Whatsoever ye bind on earth shall be bound in heaven; and whatsoever ye loose on earth shall be loosed in heaven" (KJV). Among my friends, this scripture was applied by saying, for instance, "Let's agree together in prayer that your marriage is going to be healed," or praying, "God, we bind the spirit of marital discord and loose love to be renewed between Mary Lou and Spencer." (Someone in my small group prayed that prayer almost word for word as I have written it here.)

These ways of looking at life and faith meet a deep need to feel secure, to feel that we are safe and life is predictable. Having a formula for dealing with every situation is a comfort, and believing that we can speak things into being as God did at creation (we are made in God's image, the teaching went, and so some of this power to speak things into being is within us) gives us a feeling of power over our circumstances. Unfortunately, circumstances do not always cooperate with our desire for neat answers. Faith is not magic, and scripture verses or phrases are not Christian versions of abracadabra.

God wills good for us, but this does not mean that life will be easy or that we will be exempt from trouble. Of course, we would not be so crass as to say that we expect God to shield us from all bad. But we seem to assume that if we serve God, we will at least have good family life, stability, and psychological well-being. As Martin Luther King, Jr., said in a sermon, we have rewritten the Great Commission to say, "Go ye into all the world, keep your blood pressure down, and lo, I will make you a well-adjusted personality."[2] In other words, we expect that there will be some fringe benefits of serving God.

Easy answers are often not true answers. The truth I was facing was hard for me, but as I struggled, I came to understand something much more important. I came to see that most of life is not answers but questions and that it is in the questions we meet God. In *Letters to a Young Poet*, Maria Ranier Rilke urges his friend to "live the questions," to live every part of life, until he comes to "love the questions themselves."[3] God isn't somewhere else, in the answers. God isn't somewhere "out there" where things are good. God is here. God isn't waiting for us in the future when we reach our goals, when we return from exile. God is doing something within us and through us now.

Jeremiah's advice to the people of Israel while they were in exile was that they build homes, plant trees, and pray for the peace of the land where they were. He told them to marry and have children. He told them not to put their lives on hold until the hard times were over. Build, plant, and pray is good advice. When we build a home, we invest in life now, where we are. When we plant trees that will bear fruit or give shade eventually, we are investing in the future. When we pray, we invest in what is eternal, remembering that what we build and what we plant are not what is most important. Jeremiah teaches me to give up the desire for neat answers, for life tied up with a bow on top, and instead to invest myself in life as it is, questions as well as answers.

Life is not closed but open. It is a process. That was a new idea for me. I had spent years believing that God had a "perfect will" for my life and that if I prayed and acted on the Holy Spirit's guidance, I would never displease God. I believed God had a distinct will about every little thing in my life and that I could find that will and do it. Something as awful as a divorce was surely proof that I had missed God's will for my life. When I said that to a friend, he stunned me by saying, "Maybe this is God's will for your life. Maybe there are some things you needed to learn that God knew you wouldn't learn any other way." How could he think that?

But the more I thought about his words, the more I considered that God might have an agenda for me that went beyond whether I was able to meet society's standards. Maybe what God wants for us is bigger than meeting cultural norms. I came to see that God wants me to love people (including myself) more than keeping the rules, more even than I love my dreams.

I have a cup that says, "Life. It's nothing like the brochure." Life is not what I expected it to be. I'm not where I expected it to be. But I have found God in the struggles, and I have discovered that life with God is a matter of relationship, not rules—which is good, since keeping all the rules is impossible for me. I was and always will be deeply flawed. I will never be able to live up to my highest ideals. I will never be able to do everything correctly and make everything come out okay. That has always been the truth. That is why I need God's grace. I am grateful that God pours it out on me and on all of us.

---

[1]Kathleen Norris, *Dakota: A Spiritual Geography* (New York: Houghton Mifflin, 1993), 86.

[2]Martin Luther King, Jr., "A Knock at Midnight" in *Strength to Love* (Philadelphia: Fortress Press, 1963), 57.

[3]Maria Ranier Rilke, *Letters to a Young Poet* (New York: Random House, 1986), 139.

CHAPTER 3

THIS WAS NOT IN THE CONTRACT!

O n the day my divorce decree was granted, I came out of the courthouse into a bright, sunny March afternoon. My attorney asked, "Well, how do you feel?"

"To tell you the truth, I feel like swinging around these lampposts. I feel like a kid out of school!" And I did. I had expected to be sad; I knew about the stages of grieving a loss, and people had told me that divorce is an intense loss. But I didn't feel sad; more than anything I felt relieved. And that sense of relief carried me through the next weeks. As I told someone, "So far, I feel great. I may walk around a corner some morning down the road and smack into a brick wall of grief, but right now I'm fine."

Actually, I thought I had probably done my grieving in advance. I had cried many tears during the time my marriage was falling apart. I had lived in denial for a long time, (the first stage of grief). I had certainly been through bargaining (another stage) as I prayed and fasted and tried every other strategy I knew to get a miracle. I had been angry at times (another stage), and during the time before I made the decision to divorce, I felt sure I had been depressed (another stage). That unrelenting heaviness in my limbs, the sense of trudging through even simple tasks, the crying—that sounds like depression. And now I assumed that I had reached the stage of acceptance. I was simply being efficient. And all those people who had such a hard time—well, they hadn't had all the years of counseling that I had. I decided that they weren't as well-adjusted as I was or they didn't have the spiritual maturity that I did. Whatever the reason, I was fine.

Then, one summer morning, I woke from the dream about digging up my corpse to realize that I was deeply, profoundly sad. I might have been through the stages of denial and bargaining, but now I had to face the pain. The sense of loss took my breath away. I had never intended to be a single parent. Growing up as I had with a frequently absentee father, I wanted more than anything for my child to live in a loving, stable, two-parent home. I had not planned to shoulder the responsibilities of parenting by myself, and I wanted our daughter Emily to be close to her father.

Of course, my former husband pointed out to me that she could have a two-parent home were it not for my stubbornness and selfishness in wanting out of the marriage. It was my fault that she was going to be scarred for life. I was the one who chose to end our marriage. And I had to agree. I had chosen this, and it was permanent. It was not that I regretted the divorce. I had done what was necessary to rescue myself; but in doing what I needed to do, I was inflicting on my child pain that would distort her life. I didn't want this for my child, and I didn't want it for myself. I was facing a life of aloneness.

And, as illogical as it sounds, I was angry with God. I had prayed and asked God to guide me before I married, and still I had gotten into a terrible mess. I had prayed, asking God to prepare me for being a wife and mother and to guide me to the man with whom I would spend the rest of my life. I had done it right, darn it, and here I was, struggling to take care of my child by myself, facing life without a partner! Why hadn't God stopped me? I had asked God to close the doors, to stop me if I was doing the wrong thing in marrying Spencer. But God let me go ahead.

The sadness deepened day by day. Without realizing it, I slipped deeper and deeper into depression. I stopped writing in my journal, stopped writing letters to my family, stopped cooking, stopped doing almost everything. On nights when I didn't have graduate school classes, I'd pick Emily up from day care and go home, give her dinner (kids are easy—hot dogs, grilled cheese, peanut butter and jelly—no need to really cook), put her to bed and try to study. I'd sit down with a book in front of me and begin reading, only to realize after two or three pages that I had no idea what I had just read.

Or I would come to myself simply staring at the book, making no attempt to read. I went to class, but it was as if I were enclosed in a bubble. Nothing got into my head. One day I missed an important appointment with an advisor about a graduate project. I completely forgot the appointment and simply did not show up. I had never done anything like that in my life. When I realized days after the appointment what I had done, I was stunned, not because I had forgotten but because it had taken me so long to realize that I had forgotten.

Then I began waking in the night, lying for hours, ruminating about the life that lay before me. It looked pretty horrible from my perspective. I found myself wondering if I could bear what I had chosen. I knew that I could not remain in a marriage that was destroying my sense of self, but could I bear this any more easily? In the back of my mind, I began to question seriously whether I could. I was afraid that the pain might be more than I could bear, and so I formulated a plan. I began collecting prescription medications, sleeping pills, which doctors are quite willing to prescribe to people in my situation, and pain pills for any minor thing. It really wasn't that difficult. I had some pain pills left from before the divorce, and I suffered periodically from migraines and had strong pain medication for that in a prescription I could have refilled whenever I needed it. When I had some dental work done, I told my dentist that I was a wimp about pain. Since I had fainted on him once as he began a dental procedure, he believed me. He gave me pain medication. I told myself that if the anguish got too bad, I could simply take all the pills and check out. I did not tell anyone, of course. I knew that talking about suicide would cause people to watch me more closely, and I was not going to give any clues. If I did it, I would at least do this right and succeed at it. I would not botch it up as I had marriage.

But I remembered all the things I'd heard about people who kill themselves, about suicide being a mortal sin because it was murder. Those ideas nagged at me. I didn't want to do something that would cost me my soul. So I found myself wondering if it really is possible to die of a broken heart. Could I hurt so much that my heart would just stop beating one night as I slept? Could I will that to happen? I began trying. I wanted to die. Like Elijah in the Old Testament, I found myself wishing for it, even asking God to make it so.

Elijah's life had become unbearable to him. He had faced the pagan prophets and defeated them, but Queen Jezebel wanted him dead. Fleeing from her, he had retreated to a cave and was hiding out. And he was despondent. The story in 1 Kings 19 tells us that he sent his servant away and was cowering, alone. I can picture him curled up in a fetal position in that cave, covering his head and wishing for death. He didn't try to hide his feelings from God. Elijah seemed to have forgotten his faith, forgotten all that God had done for him in the past. He had just come from a dramatic showdown with the prophets of Baal, but what was in the past didn't matter. He was having a crisis of faith. The erstwhile prophet and hero was little more than a quivering mass of emotions—fear, depression, withdrawal. And what did God do? God sent an angel who took care of Elijah (1 Kings 19:5, 7). Then God spoke to him—not in the earthquake or the fire or the wind but in what the New Revised Standard Version describes as "sheer silence" (v.12). (We have more familiarly heard it called a "still, small voice" (KJV). Whatever it was, it was not something dramatic and showy.

This picture of God softens my heart. God does not tell Elijah to get hold of himself, to pull himself together and get a grip, to shake it off and start acting like a prophet. First, God takes care of Elijah's physical needs, sending angels to care for him and food to strengthen him. Then God tenderly speaks to him. Here is a God who understands our fears, who watches over us when we are in despair, who takes the initiative in reaching out to us when we are overwhelmed by our pain.

And that is how God dealt with me. God sent angels to care for me. The first one didn't look much like those angels we see in paintings. He was a big guy from Georgia who loved sports. His name was Ken Jones, and he stopped me in the hall at the church, where he was also a part-time staffer.

Ken knew about my divorce, and he asked me how things were going. We talked for only a minute or two, but he asked me to come by his office later in the week. When I did, he asked whether I had gone to the singles Sunday school class at the church. I had not. Most of the people in the class were older than I, in their forties and fifties. Besides, I was still hiding out, rarely leaving my house except to go to school and work. Ken said, "We need another class for younger singles. Would you help me get one started?" I agreed, somewhat reluctantly. I don't know if Ken sensed my despair or if he was just doing his job in trying to help the church grow, but whether he knew it or not, he called me out of the cave that I had retreated into emotionally. It was a soft call, one I could have ignored. But his expression of caring made a difference. That was the beginning of a change for me. We put a notice in the church paper and made a few calls, and in a few weeks I found myself surrounded by another group of angels, probably one of the unlikeliest groups of angels you could imagine.

One was a young woman who had recently become a Christian. A long-term relationship had ended, and she moved back to Tulsa to be near her family. Another was a young woman who had come to town to join her husband in his new job, only to have him announce after she arrived that he had fallen in love with a co-worker and wanted a divorce. Another was a man who had come to town to attend seminary, decided seminary was not for him, and now was struggling to find God's direction for his life. Another was a woman whose husband had left her for another man several years earlier. These people and the others in the class did what the

United Methodist baptismal vows say we will do: they surrounded me with "a community of love and forgiveness." We formed the nucleus of a Sunday school class that included sometimes just a few others and sometimes as many as thirty people.

We were not poster kids for the American dream, I have to admit. We were hurting and needy. But somehow God acted among us and through us. These people pulled me back from the edge; with their help, I began to emerge from the darkness. I came to be able to call on any of them at any hour of the day or night—and I did, after a nightmare, or when I woke crying from dreams I couldn't even remember. When I felt like I couldn't drag myself out of the house, one of them would call and say, "Let's go to Diamond Jack's to eat," or, "Some of us are getting together for potluck at Carolyn's. Grab something and come over." When I needed help with Emily on the spur of the moment or when my car broke down, they stepped in. Looking back, I know quite surely that God sent them into my life. They fed me, literally and figuratively. They were God's way of helping me to see that even when life is far from what we want it to be, it is still worth living. And they didn't do it by telling me that. They did it by being honest about their own struggles and crying about their pain. They did it by making me laugh at our horrible stories of what it was like to be in the messes we were in. I cared about them; I saw them for the gifted and wonderful people they were, and I saw God at work through them. For me, they were a sign of hope and proof that God's grace flows through even broken vessels.

One night as Jennifer and I sat on my sofa talking, I began crying, telling her that I felt like the pain was going to crush the life out of me, that it was like it was never going to stop hurting. She said, "Mary Lou, one of the great lies of the universe is that things are always going to be just like they are today. Don't believe it. It's not true." Her words went right to my heart. They were exactly what I needed to hear. I needed to understand that the pain wasn't going to go on forever, that it would end. As my senior social studies teacher in high school told us often, "Remember, good or bad, this too shall pass." Pain can blind us to everything beyond the moment, and I was giving in to the great lie that life is only pain and grief. I began to consider the possibility that my life would change for the better. I didn't have any evidence for it, but if Jenny could believe it in her situation, I could try to believe it in mine. She was God's messenger—God's angel—to me that night. So I trudged on, trying to read the Bible, trying to pray, trying to believe.

One Saturday morning late in summer, as I was looking for something in the refrigerator, I came across my cache of pain pills and sleeping pills. I said to myself, "This is dangerous. Emily could get into these. What was I thinking?" I took the bottles into the bathroom, dumped the contents into the toilet, and flushed it. As I watched the tablets and capsules swirling down the drain, I realized I had turned a corner. I didn't want to die any more. Don't get me wrong. Life wasn't rosy; I wasn't all smiles. Externally, nothing much was different. I was still concerned about Emily and how I was going to rear her, about how I was going to pay the bills, about facing life alone. But I had stopped planning on checking out. I felt a vague inkling of a desire to tackle life again.

As I was studying the Bible one night with some other singles, a verse from 1 Peter 5 jumped out at me. The verse says the God of all grace will "restore, support, strengthen, and establish you" (1 Pet. 5:10). It was as if God were saying to me personally, "You're not going to recover from this instantly. It's a process. We'll take it one step at a time." I realized that first God would have to "restore" me—mend me, take care of the brokenness. Then God would make me strong and, eventually, stable. And God would hold me up while all this was going on. I copied that verse onto a card and fastened it to the refrigerator door with magnets, right at eye level. Day after day, every time I read that verse, I reminded myself that I had to be patient, that God was working on me.

When depression comes, the rest of the world doesn't stop. I struggled to continue functioning. But even when we retreat into our caves, God is at work deep within us. Changes are happening even when we are not able to see them, and even when I couldn't see progress, the verse from First Peter helped me to trust that there was some. Depression doesn't go away instantly and permanently all at once, and I began participating in singles activities while I was still depressed, deeply wounded, and needy. I wasn't okay. I didn't understand the deep process of healing that needed to happen within me. But each invitation to take part in some activity was God offering me a morsel. Sometimes I took it; sometimes I did not.

At the end of Elijah's time in the wilderness, God told him to go and seek out Elisha. Looking at the story now, I believe God was telling Elijah something very important: that he needed someone to help him. It was a critical time for Elijah personally and in his ministry, and God directed him to reach out. Elijah had something to do for God, but he was not to try to go it alone, at least not during this time in his life. Some things we can do for ourselves, but in times of pain and loss, we need others to help us. Elijah needed just one other person. Some of us need more than one person. Some turn to family or friends, but some of us don't feel comfortable talking with them. I was one of those. Divorce and grief recovery groups offer the special benefit of anonymity. At times it is easier to talk with strangers, people we don't have to see in other settings, than with family or friends who are grieving over our divorce too. I found that there was great comfort and encouragement in being with those who were going through the same struggles I was facing, and I found my greatest help within the community of faith.

As the months passed, I was able to look outward a little more. That didn't mean I always found it easy to enter singles functions or that I felt happy. Moving back into relating to people was like physical therapy after an injury. It was painful, but it was necessary for me to regain my strength and mobility. So I forced myself to speak to people, to sign up for special events, to attend seminars. Every time I went to one of them, I'd meet someone who was a little further along in their process of recovering from loss than I was and also someone who was where I had been earlier. Or I'd hear about a book that someone found helpful. I'd get one little idea or strategy that would move me a little further along my path, and I'd feel better. I'd find myself thinking, "I'm doing okay with this. I'm pulling out of the funk. This is almost over." And then I'd wake up one morning depressed again, the world looking dismal and me feeling hopeless.

The stages of grief are not sequential and neat. I moved in and out of them, including depression. It felt like the old three-steps-forward-two-steps-back routine. But eventually the times of feeling down didn't last as long. The depression was less intense, and I seemed to recover my energy and initiative more quickly after each bout with it.

One of the coping skills I learned during this time was to pay attention to things that might trigger depression. Special days like holidays are a challenge after a loss. I knew it would be important for me not to be alone, so I took care to plan in advance. The first year, I went out of town for both Thanksgiving and Christmas. Facing these times in the home I'd shared with Spence did not seem wise. But I also did not want to be with my family. I felt too much guilt over my failure, and I hadn't been with them on these holidays for years. Being with close friends was more fun, and I felt supported by their love.

I was prepared for the holidays. What I was not prepared for was the other special days and how they might affect me. In a meeting one night I mentioned feeling anxious, short-tempered, and tense. I caught myself about to make a snide comment to another group member and said instead, "I don't know what's wrong with me! I feel like I could hit someone or dissolve into tears—and I'm not sure which."

A woman sitting near me said, "Is some special day coming up—an anniversary, or your birthday or something?" The day that would have been my wedding anniversary was only a few days away. I hadn't even been conscious of that until I heard the question. That incident taught me to pay attention to the calendar. My birthday, Spencer's birthday, the anniversary of the day I got my engagement ring—any of them could set off an episode of sadness. But being aware of that helped me to take better care of myself.

Another way of taking care of myself was so basic that I hesitate to mention it: Getting regular exercise and adequate rest and eating right. These are important for me all the time but especially so at stressful times like holidays and anniversaries. People who had been through struggles like mine reminded me of that. Exercise drained off some of the anger that I still struggled with at times, and I am grateful for friends who scheduled regular racquetball games. They did not allow me to forget to take care of myself, and physical exhaustion is also a wonderful sleep aid. Forming new habits in these areas helped me to emerge from the pattern of depression.

Elijah's despair and my own taught me that God doesn't give up on us when we retreat into our anguish and try to hide from life. When we are ready to give up on ourselves, grace is there, persistent, even stubborn. God sends whatever messengers are available, with some morsel to nourish us and help us keep going. And God calls to us until we are able to listen. As to Elijah slinking out of that cave, God speaks to us. What God says may not be what we expect to hear, and at first we may think God is silent. But God does speak. And as we listen, God leads us out of despair and enables us to face life again. The challenges don't disappear for us any more than they did for Elijah, but I have come to believe that God loves a challenge and can't resist getting in there with us when we face one. That's one of the ways grace intersects our lives.

CHAPTER 4

OLD PATTERNS, NEW WOUNDS

O ne of the things I love most about the people in Bible stories is that they are real people. They aren't perfect, and the stories don't attempt to present them as perfect. My favorite dysfunctional Bible family is Jacob and Esau's. What we hear about the perpetuation of patterns of abuse within families becomes more understandable when we look closely at Laban, Rebekah, Jacob, Esau, Rachel, and Leah. You probably remember some of the story—Jacob and Esau are twins, and Jacob cheats Esau out of his birthright in a deal involving a bowl of stew. But when we look closely at what happens before and after the bowl-of-stew incident between the brothers, we should not be surprised that there was trouble.

Jacob's name means "Usurper" or "Deceiver," but that might as well be the family name for the entire clan. Those who know the Bible story usually remember that Jacob was a trickster, but we may not realize where he learned this behavior. Rebekah, Jacob's mother, helped him cook up the plot to deceive Isaac on his deathbed and get the blessing reserved for the firstborn. Rebekah was, in fact, behind the scenes directing much of what went on. She was an eavesdropper (Gen. 27:5) and a liar (Gen. 27:45) as well a manipulator and a schemer. She was the one who told Jacob to get the calf to cook into a stew; she was the one who arranged for the animal skins he wore as a disguise to convince his father that he was the hirsute brother. Rebekah was the one who came up with a plan to get Jacob out of town so his angry brother would not kill him after their father died. Rebekah was an operator, a practiced deceiver, and I doubt that her machinations around Isaac's deathbed were new behavior. She had probably been doing things like this for years, and her son had been watching.

To be fair to Rebekah, she was not the only deceiver in the family. Isaac lied about Rebekah's identity too, at one point, saying she was his sister rather than his wife (Gen. 26:7). Deceit was a family pattern. Jacob didn't become a deceiver by accident. He learned to be the kind of person he was, and like most of us, he probably learned this behavior and his other ways of dealing with life from his family.

The deceit goes beyond these three. Genesis 29–31 tells the story of Jacob going to his mother's homeland to find a wife. He goes to work for Laban, an older uncle. Jacob falls in love with Rachel, the younger of Laban's daughters, and agrees to work for seven years to earn the privilege of marrying her. At the end of the seven years, on the wedding night Laban slips his older daughter Leah into the tent instead of Rachel. There being no electric lights in the desert, Jacob doesn't know he is sleeping with the wrong sister until the morning—and by then it is too late. When he confronts Laban about the deception, Laban tells Jacob that he couldn't allow Rachel to marry before her older sister. This was not something Laban had just discovered; he had known it all along. As he told Jacob, it was their custom. When the time came, he did what he had been planning to do.

When Jacob and his two wives are preparing to leave Laban, Jacob and Laban engage in mutual trickery regarding how they will divide the livestock. Later, instead of taking their leave openly, Jacob and his wives slip away secretly without saying good-bye. Before they go, Rachel steals household gods from her father and lies to him when he comes after their caravan to retrieve them. In this family, lying and scheming and deceiving are entrenched behavior. It is their way. Generation after generation, it is their way.

As I think about this family, I think of the scripture about the "sins of the fathers" being visited on the children "unto the third and fourth generations." This is not a curse in the sense that God punishes children for what their great-grandparents did. That is not God's nature. But all of us are the products of our upbringing. When we live by patterns that are damaging, we learn (and teach) ways of coping with life that may damage us and our children after us and their children after them—and that makes four generations.

What happens in our families becomes the norm for us, the way the world is. Often we do not realize that what is going on is suspect or even unusual. I once was in a small group where we told one another stories about our upbringing as a way of getting to know one another. One woman in the group told us that she had one sister and that theirs had been an ordinary, unremarkable childhood. Later, in the course of talking about something else, she told a story of sitting on the sofa with her mother and sister while her father fired shots into the wall above their heads. I could not believe what I was hearing! This was an unremarkable childhood? For her, something as incredible and dangerous as firing a gun at one's family was unremarkable.

Sometimes in our families we learn to accept and ignore outrageous behavior as if it were nothing to be concerned about. In recovery groups, I have heard this is called "ignoring the purple elephant sitting in the middle of the living room." Families ignore or cover for members' behaviors such as addiction or abuse and keep it a family secret. This is not a new pattern of behavior discovered by the recovery movement. An old movie called *Papa's Delicate Condition* dealt with alcoholism. When the father of the family was too drunk to participate in his family's life, the mother told the children, "Papa's not feeling well." Many alcoholics are described as "ill" or "under the weather," and the "illness" is never discussed outside the home.

Some of us lived with similar purple elephants in the middle of our living rooms, never acknowledging some huge reality such as abuse or illness or financial catastrophe that affected our family life. We all also lived with less spectacular realities such as ways of relating to one another that shape our relationships. In my family, I learned that no matter what a husband did, in Mother's opinion the wife should be loyal to him. She grew up in a patriarchal culture where men beat their wives and children if they misbehaved. Children and women were the property of their husbands and fathers, and outsiders did not interfere in another family's private affairs. The theology in that culture said divorce is wrong. Divorce was permissible only in cases of adultery. And even adultery (on the part of men—adulterous women were rare and might be beaten to death by their husbands) was often forgiven, tolerated, or overlooked. My parents were not Christian and never attended church, but somehow they still absorbed these ideas from the people around them in Appalachia.

Layered on top of this was the culture of the South, from which I learned that women should not be direct. Women took care of others, ignoring their own needs and wants if necessary. Both my mother and mother-in-law found it almost impossible to be direct, even about inconsequential things. Once when my mother-in-law was visiting, I asked while making the grocery list, "Do you like smooth peanut butter or crunchy?"

"Oh, whatever you all want is fine with me."

"Do you have a preference? I'll be glad to get whichever you want. We eat both."

"No, no, you just get whatever you want."

"Okay, then. I'll get crunchy this time because I got smooth last time." She looked a bit disappointed, so (having also been trained as Southern females are to read the slightest cues of facial expression or emotion) I asked, "Are you sure that's okay with you?" (Another Southern female thing, pull the information out of them if that's what it takes.)

"Well, I really do prefer smooth." It was just peanut butter. Why couldn't she simply state her preference? Because it is unladylike to be direct. A lady is always sweet, soft-spoken, gracious, and deferential. She had been reared to be cooperative, pleasant, and undemanding.

My mother was much the same. Once when she was visiting in my home, Mother said, "A big glass of ice water sure would taste good right now." She was thirsty, but she could not ask for what she wanted. These women could not be direct with me about something as simple as peanut butter or a glass of water. You can imagine how circuitously they dealt with weightier matters. Women like these had been my models for dealing with life.

This trait alone would be a handicap in relationships. Unfortunately, it does not stop with the way we express ourselves. Women learn to use indirect means to get what they want and need. My friend Renee told me about her family and the way they ate on holidays. When the clan of eight siblings and spouses and children gathered at her grandmother's house, the dining room could not accommodate everyone. So the men ate first. Then the women and children ate. Renee quickly saw the inequity of this arrangement and brought it to her mother's attention. Her mother simply told her that this was the way it was. But Renee, having been reared somewhat differently than those in the older generation, would not leave the subject alone. Year after year, she asked her mother why it was allowed to continue. Finally, when Renee was about fifteen, her mother apparently decided it was time to let her in on the secret. She took Joyce into the kitchen while the men were eating and opened the oven door. She asked Joyce, "What do you see?"

"I see part of a ham and part of a roast."

"No, what you see is the loin of the ham and the roast. We keep this for ourselves. The men don't get the best." She was partly right; the men weren't getting the best. But neither were the women. When people deceive each other in their daily interactions, no one gets the best that relationships have to offer.

These stories illustrate basics of the way we Southern women are taught to interact with men. Like Scarlett O'Hara making a dress out of curtains and attempting to convince Rhett Butler that all was well at Tara, we are taught to use backdoor ways to get what we want and need, while appearing to observe the conventions. Never mind that there's deception in it. For good or ill, the women and men close to us become our models for how to fill our roles.

In my family, there were different rules for women and men about many things. For instance, my father was a philanderer. As far back as I can remember, he had affairs. He left my mother and us children many times. Sometimes he would be gone for months, even a year. But Dad was not only a philanderer; he was also cruel about it. In later years, when as Mother put it he would "take up with some woman," he would flaunt his infidelity. Many times he came to our house to pick up his mail or some clothes and brought along his current paramour. I remember seeing one of these women sitting in his car at the curb, silhouetted against the afternoon sun as she smoked a cigarette. He always made sure that Mother knew that there was another woman. That was a part of the game. After these humiliations, Mother would retreat to her bedroom. She would come out eventually, eyes red from crying, and go on as if nothing were wrong.

Eventually Dad would come home, asking forgiveness, and always Mother would extend it. I could not understand how she could allow him to return, but year after year, she did. And each time he returned, for a while our household would be relatively calm. But when they argued, Dad would point out to Mother how badly she compared to other women. I remember her saying to him in tears during one argument, "But I didn't know."

"Well, you should have known!" he yelled, encapsulating in those few words his standard view that she was responsible for whatever the problem was. To my amazement, Mother seemed to accept his evaluations. She seemed to believe that if she could do things differently, he would be different. It was her fault that our home wasn't happy, and I could tell from what she said and how she looked that she felt worthless. Those times when he left us, she kept our home as stable as she could, working multiple jobs to provide for us. She was the reliable one, the one who made sure we had food and clothes.

Seeing how Mother suffered from my dad's emotional cruelty and physical abuse, I vowed that I would never allow any man to mistreat me. One of the ways that I would avoid that, of course, was to marry a Christian. It seemed self-evident that a Christian would never harm me as I saw Dad harming Mother.

As I had continued in counseling to unlearn some of the patterns that limited me, I was direct with Spencer about what I needed or felt. I was not being the undemanding, indirect Southern woman he wanted. One afternoon, as I spoke to him about some minor issue, he became suddenly and explosively angry. For just an instant, I thought he was about to hit me. That was it. I said, "You are angry all out of proportion to what is going on here. I don't know what the anger is about, and you may not either, but you have to get help in dealing with it. I will not stay with anyone as angry as you are."

I was very clear that I would not place myself or our child in a setting that might lead to violence. I had seen and experienced enough violence in my home while I was growing up to know that it only escalates. I knew the terror of being a helpless child, and when I thought Spencer was about to hit me, that terror came back.[1] I am just over five feet tall; he was several inches over six feet and outweighed me by well over 100 pounds. I felt unsafe, and I was unwilling to stay in that situation. That pattern was one I had consciously decided long before to break, and when his anger frightened me, I knew what I had to do. I had decided to protect myself and my child or children if I ever found myself in danger of abuse, and I found it easy to speak out. I insisted that Spencer see a counselor, which he did— for a few sessions. My fear became a catalyst for change.

There was no physical abuse in my marriage, but near the end of it Spencer was in so much pain that he sometimes lashed out at me verbally when I tried to reach out to him in comfort or friendship. It came to the point that nothing I did was right, nothing I said was right. We were both like wounded animals, volatile and unable to help one another because of our own pain. But it was fear for my physical safety that got my attention.

What astounded me in looking back at our marriage later was that I had not recognized the pattern of blaming and humiliation that I was caught in. I was beaten down as much as my mother had been. I had accepted Spencer's evaluations of me, and I had accepted blame for his unhappiness as well as my own. But I could not see it. Though Spencer was not a violent and physically abusive alcoholic as my father had been, the emotional dynamic between us was the same one my parents had lived by. I had chosen or created a situation like the one I grew up in. I accepted Spence's statements that I was the problem, that I was the one who needed counseling. I had accepted the "Well, you should have known!" verdict, just as Mother had. I should have known; I should have been able to fix it. And also like Mother, I had done my crying in private and pretended to those around me that nothing was wrong. But no matter what I did it would never be enough. I saw that if I stayed with him, we would continue playing out the script that had characterized my parents' relationship.[2]

The moment I came to that insight, I realized that Spencer was not the first man of his type in my life. Looking back on men I had dated, it was clear that I had chosen and attracted others like him, men who wanted not a partner and friend but someone who would take care of all their needs, putting aside her own needs no matter what the cost. Once I saw this, I knew that I had to stop the cycle. If my daughter was to learn healthy models of relating, I would have to change.

As I looked carefully at my marriage, I realized that I had lived all my life trying to please others, trying to figure out what they wanted and then to be that. From my teachers in school to my parents to my husband, I had shaped my life according to what I thought would please others.[3] I felt overwhelmed by this insight. I would have to change my entire way of relating. But as Luke 12:48 says, "From everyone to whom much has been given, much will be required." Having been given insight into these unhealthy patterns, I was required to live differently in the future. God's grace was at work, calling me to face the past, calling me toward wholeness.

Going back to the story of Jacob's family in Genesis, I see a change in Jacob that helps me think in new ways about this. Years after Jacob left his home, he decided to go back. He decided to face his brother and what he had done. Chapters 32 and 33 of Genesis tell the story of the brothers being reunited. Jacob decides to face Esau. He sends envoys ahead with gifts to placate his brother. After wrestling with God's messenger through the night, when the morning comes he moves forward. Jacob prepares for the worst, fearing that Esau might send warriors to attack him and his entourage. So Jacob divides his livestock into two groups and arranges his wives and children in ranks. The least favorite ones are placed at the front of the caravan, and the most favored wife Rachel is with her son Joseph at the end of the line, most protected from harm. What we see here is a frightened man. What he is doing is not easy, and he fears that they all will suffer.

When I decided to face my past, when I decided to admit that I had been living by damaging patterns, I was afraid. I didn't know any other way to live; I didn't know any way to relate other than the indirect and manipulative way I had learned, and familiar misery is often easier than the unknown. Those dark times of my marriage ending were my times of wrestling with God, though like Jacob I did not realize for a long while that it was God with whom I wrestled. God was coming to me in many ways through many people, asking me to look at what was going on, to see what I needed to do, and trying to strengthen me to do it. Finally I became willing to face the unwholesome patterns, to name them for what they were.

In the Genesis story, when Jacob turned, he found a brother more willing to forgive him than he was to forgive himself. He said, in fact, that seeing his brother's face was "like seeing the face of God" (Gen. 33:10, TEV).

In a similar way, when I turned to face the destructive patterns that I wanted to transform, I found myself looking into the face of God, who was graciously waiting to receive me, more ready to heal me and to help me than I ever expected.

Giving up one way of life for another is always scary. I did not know what was going to happen, and I wasn't sure what was ahead for me. Could I learn to interact openly and honestly with people, without trying to manipulate them into doing what I wanted and needed them to do? If I gave up trying to say what I thought people wanted to hear and do what they wanted me to do, would they accept me for the person I was?

They were tough questions, and I did not have answers. I wish I could tell you that I was instantly changed, that in a moment all the old ways disappeared and I was able to relate to others in the ways I felt God wanted me to. But most changes don't happen that way, and mine didn't either. The insight about the old, hurtful patterns came as a flash, but the changes in behavior came bit by bit, day by day. In fact, the first step toward them was a request from my counselor to be part of a group he was forming. It involved reading books and meeting weekly, and it didn't really look much like a miracle. I was in graduate school and busy already, and his request looked suspiciously like more work. I told him I'd think about it. As I did, I remembered my pain over the way I had related to Spencer, and I decided to invest time and energy in the group. I needed someone to help me, to coach me in relating to others. What I needed was a relationship lab, the way high school kids have a chemistry lab and a teacher looking over their shoulder, helping them with the experiments. Ben, my counselor, promised that was what the class would be, that the others were people like me who were there to work on their ways of dealing with others.

Though it was not a divorce recovery group, several the people in the group were divorced or divorcing. Ben believed we could help each other. It felt strange. We met and talked about what seemed to me trivial things at first, relating in superficial ways as we talked about the readings. One night someone wore to class a tee shirt that had a cartoon of a fish on a bicycle, pedaling with its fins. The caption on the tee shirt said a man is as unnecessary to a woman as a bicycle is to a fish. Dick, one of the class members, agreed with that sentiment, saying we all had to get past needing relationships. I thought the cartoon was hostile and harsh—but I said nothing. Sometime later I mentioned to Ben that I hoped the subject would come up again in class so I could tell Dick that I disagreed with the hostile tone of that cartoon (and many of the jokes that were bandied back and forth). Ben said, "You don't have to wait for it to come up. Why can't you just say to Dick, 'I've been thinking about that t-shirt discussion, and I wanted to say something to you about it"? As remarkable as it sounds, it had not occurred to me to bring up the subject in order to let Dick know what I thought. That would not be a Southern-female thing to do. I did not express my opinions about potentially divisive subjects, and in that group the subject of male-female relationships could be very divisive. My conversation with Ben showed me how basic the changes would need to be, and I began practicing in my daily conversations.

It was torture. I wanted people to like me—all people. I wanted to be acceptable and accepted. If I said what I really thought, if I did not edit my responses and behavior continually, I might offend someone or cause someone to evaluate me negatively. Could I risk being honest? Could I risk being direct? To do less would be dishonest—and I was sure God was not in favor of dishonesty. But that did not make it easy for me to make the changes. And this was only one area where I needed to change!

The process reminds me of a poster I once saw. It pictured a rag doll halfway through the wringers of an old washer. Adding to John 8:32, the caption said that although the truth makes us free, it also will first make us uncomfortable. Quite often as I struggled to change, I was miserable. I was giving up my familiar way of dealing with others, and I was not sure what I was supposed to use to replace it. But God was there, coaxing me along, stopping me in the middle of a sentence and reminding me to be honest, to be myself. And I was learning and changing, bit by bit. It was like looking into the face of God and seeing there a smile of understanding and encouragement.

There were other patterns I had to confront too. I had to learn to acknowledge my anger and express it without becoming verbally abusive toward the person whose behavior I disliked. Verbal abuse had been common in my family, and I was slowly becoming aware of its lingering effect on me.[4] I have a strong tendency to resort to sarcasm, and my language can become very strong. Though I am not physically violent, I still struggle not to use violent metaphors in expressing what I feel. I grew up hearing things like, "Do you want a beating? That's exactly what you're going to get if you keep that up," and, "Do that one more time and I'll knock you clean into the middle of next week!" I have come to see that language like "How does that strike you?" and "shut up" and "I could just choke her!" are verbal violence. It is everywhere in our culture, and it is hard not to give in to using it. I continue trying to avoid it.

I had to learn to state my wishes and wants instead of trying to manipulate people into doing what I want. I had to learn to ask for what I need rather than hoping people would somehow magically figure it out. I had to learn to accept responsibility when I did something wrong. But I also had to learn that if someone was upset, I was not necessarily to blame. For me, that was really tough. If someone was angry or sad, I always wanted to fix it, to make them feel okay again. I had to learn that I cannot "fix" other people.

There is a passage of scripture that offered me a new insight into this process of facing the past. It's in chapter 21 of the Book of Numbers. The people of Israel are being bitten by serpents, and many of them are dying. Moses is told by God to make a bronze serpent and mount it on a pole. Those who have been bitten are to look at the bronze serpent, and when they do so, they are healed. I thought of how we are sometimes told that when we face our fears and faults "we take the first step tworad overcoming them." Maybe the same is true of the things that damage us. When the Israelites turned to look squarely at what had harmed them, they began to get better. When Jacob went back to face his brother and what he had done, he was changed. Maybe it is only as we face squarely the damaging patterns of our past and name them for what they are that we can be free. Identifying the behaviors that have limited and harmed us in the past can become the door into a healthier life. As I recognized destructive patterns in my past and named them for what they were, that began my healing from them.

I want my guiding principle in dealing with people to be Ephesians 4:14-15: "We must no longer be children, tossed to and fro and blown about by every wind of doctrine, by people's trickery, by their craftiness in deceitful scheming. But speaking the truth in love, we must grow up in every way into him who is the head, into Christ." "Speaking the truth in love" is a tough standard, one I don't always meet. Often I speak the truth witheringly, with very little love. Sometimes speaking the truth is hard because I have to say things that people don't want to hear, things that I don't really want to say. But especially within the community of faith, we need to hear the truth. God speaks to us through one another, and when we speak the truth in love, we participate in the process of helping one another grow into the fullness of Christ. God is still working on me. The passage from Ephesians says we are to grow up into Christ "in every way," and I feel sure I haven't discovered all the ways I need to change.

The old patterns are deeply ingrained, and I easily fall back into old ways of relating. The Holy Spirit nudges me often and reminds me to pay attention, and I need that. I am like the blind man in the Gospel story (Mark 8:22-26) who is only partly healed the first time Jesus touches him. Jesus asks the man whether he can see clearly (I'd probably have been tempted to assure Jesus I could see fine, because I would have assumed that's what he wanted to hear), and he tells Jesus he can see movement but that people look like trees walking. Jesus then prays for the man again. My damaging patterns are not wiped out all at once. I have to come back again and again and ask God to touch me again, to bring me closer to complete healing.

God always wants us to love ourselves and care for ourselves. That is the foundation of loving others. Healthy self-love teaches us that each of us is a dearly loved child of God, someone to be honored and respected. We do not deserve and should not tolerate abuse of any kind. God cherishes us and wills for us loving relationships where we are valued, honored, and supported in finding abundant life. In order to find these good relationships, we have to turn and face the past. We have to be willing to name the destructive patterns we see and to change them. Whether the pattern goes back two generations or ten, God gives us the power to change. The misery we feel in the process may be our time of wrestling with God. The wrestling ended with a blessing for Jacob, and it can be so for us as well.

---

[1]There are many books that address the issue of repeating in adulthood patterns learned in childhood. Some that I'm familiar with are *Your Inner Child of the Past* by W. Hugh Missildine (Simon and Schuster, 1991); *Growing Up Again: Transactional Analysis with Gestalt Experiments* by Jean Illsley Clark and Connie Dawson (Hazledon Foundation, 1989); *Unlocking the Secrets of Your Childhood Memories* by Kevin Leman and Randy Carlson (Pocket Books, 1990); *Homecoming: Reclaiming and Championing Your Inner Child* by John Bradshaw

(Bantam Books, 1992); *The Family Patterns Workbook: Breaking Free from Your Past and Creating a Life of Your Own* by Carolyn Foster (Putnam, 1993); and *Inner Child Workbook: What to Do with Your Past When It Just Won't Go Away* by Cathryn L. Taylor (Putnam, 1991).

[2]The concept of scripting is explained in detail in Muriel James' and Dorothy Jongeward's book *Born to Win* 4th ed.(Addison Wesley Longman, 1996).

[3]If this is a pattern hampering you, you may want to look at *Pleasing You Is Destroying Me: How to Stop Being Controlled by Your People-pleasing Addictions* by Bobbie Reed (Word, 1992).

[4]For more information on this, see *Verbal Abuse: Healing the Hidden Wound* by Grace H. Ketterman (Servant Publications, 1993).

CHAPTER 5

LEARNING TO LEAN

I sat in a graduate seminar classroom, working during our thirty-minute break on balancing my checkbook and trying to figure out which bills to pay and which could wait. As I busily tallied columns of figures, one of my classmates asked, "What are you doing?"

"Trying to figure out which bills to pay. It's a classic case of too much month at the end of the money."

"I thought once you were married you didn't have to worry about that any more." Like most graduate students we were financially challenged, but JoAnne was single, struggling to pay tuition and living expenses on her own. She thought since I was married I wouldn't have to struggle as much. I had thought the same thing. Of course that wasn't true, but now that I had a child and was divorcing I was facing an even more intense struggle.

One of the truths about divorce is that the standard of living usually goes down for the woman and her children. I was no exception. I was completely on my own. After a divorce many women find themselves juggling payments and worrying about next month's mortgage while also dealing with the pain of losing the primary relationship in their lives. I could hardly concentrate on anything, and I was facing more financial responsibilities and liabilities than ever in my life. I felt scared and alone and very vulnerable.

Of course the temptation is to say, "Just trust God." But those three short words are a weighty load. I grew up in a home where trusting was tough. Because of my dad's alcoholism and the resulting erratic behavior, we could never count on his income being available. It was an unpredictable and frightening way to live. Sometimes Dad would not come home on the night he got paid. When he eventually did come home, drunk, he often would have spent his paycheck, without even knowing where or how. I had seen Mother crying in worry because there was no money for food or rent. She cleaned houses for various people in our town on a day-to-day basis, and many days she would not have money to buy food for our supper until she was paid for that day's work. I was intimately familiar with insecurity about basic needs being met.

Now, day after day I found myself reliving the feelings of terror and vulnerability that I had felt so often as a child. Though I was a grown-up, inside I felt like a six-year-old who was hungry and didn't know if there would be supper. It didn't matter that I had a job (three jobs, actually, all part-time); I was afraid and unsure. My former husband's family was wealthy, and I had thought when I married him that I was guaranteed stability and freedom from want. I had believed insecurity would be a thing of the past. I very much wanted it to be.

Instead I found myself wondering how I would take care of Emily and myself. Then I lost one of my part-time jobs. I nearly panicked. Like the widow of Zarephath in the Bible (the story is in 1 Kings 17) who could not provide for her child, I could see no way out for us. I had limited resources, and my family was not in a position to help. What was I going to do?

In the Bible story, the Lord sends the prophet Elijah to the widow's home. A part of understanding the story and how desperate she felt is understanding the position of widows in that society. Since there were few jobs for women except prostitution, respectable women were dependent on their fathers and later their husbands for shelter, protection, and whatever else they needed. When a woman's husband died and she was childless, she married his brother in order to have a child to be her first husband's heir. (This was called levirate marriage; the husband's family was expected to protect his property—Deuteronomy 25:5-10—and producing an heir was a part of that.) If there was no brother, some more distant relative might marry the widow, as Boaz did in the Book of Ruth. But the Widow of Zarephath had a son, so there was no obligation on the part of her husband's brothers to marry her. If she had been the daughter of a priest, she might have returned to her father's home or a brother's (Leviticus 22:13), but for some reason this widow apparently had no one to return to.

Being a widow was not a respected position. When we read between the lines in Hebrew scripture, we see some troublesome attitudes. The Israelites believed that bad fortune was often a sign of sin. For a widow, losing her husband could be interpreted as punishment for something she had done; or some might believe he died as punishment for some sin he committed. There is a story in Genesis 38 about Er, a son of Judah, and his widow Tamar. Genesis 38:7 says that Er "was wicked in the sight of the LORD, and the LORD put him to death." Her husband's wickedness was the cause of Tamar's widowhood. The Widow of Zarephath may have believed that her situation was God's judgment. She probably felt censure from those around her; perhaps she felt guilty and ashamed as well as frightened and vulnerable. Perhaps she felt disgraced. Isaiah 54:4 includes as part of a promise of restoration, "You will forget the shame of your youth, and the disgrace of your widowhood you will remember no more." The Widow of Zarephath later accuses Elijah of coming there "to bring my sin to my remembrance" (1 Kings 17:18), as if her widowhood and her son's later illness are some form of punishment. In her mind at least, the hard times she was facing were signals to those around her that she had done something wrong. Add to this uncertainty about whether her and her son's daily needs would be met, and I see someone I can identify with. Disgraced by the failure of my marriage, I felt that many people thought I deserved what I was getting, that I could have avoided this by staying married.

It was the widow and her child, just the two of them, and there was a famine in their country. Though we don't know how long she had been struggling, it was long enough that the food was almost gone. She was at the end of her meager supply of meal, and she was at the end of her hope. When Elijah approached her and asked her to give him some water and "a morsel of bread" (1 Kings 17:11), her first response was to refuse. "I have only enough to make a few cakes for my son and me, and then we will eat them and die," she said (AP). But something caused her to change her mind. What might have been going through her mind? Did Elijah's certainty that God would provide awaken hope in her? Or was he so forceful that she felt intimidated and did what he asked without really wanting to? We don't know. All we know is that she did what he asked. Hers was not an enthusiastic, faith-filled response. It was tentative, but it was probably all she could manage. I know that feeling too. And she used the last of the meal to make bread for them. Picture the widow as she went to sleep that night. Maybe she berated herself for squandering their last food. Maybe she lay awake trying to figure out where she could borrow some food the next day. But maybe she lay there with just a tiny spark of expectancy. Maybe she believed that Elijah's arrival signaled a change, that God had taken notice of her situation and was going to intervene. I like to think that she was able to open herself to possibility, to the idea that God was about to do something. She might have fallen asleep that night saying, "Maybe, just maybe. . . ."

That's not how I fell asleep. In fact, some nights I could hardly sleep at all for worrying about how I would provide for us. On top of the unpaid bills, I also struggled with hearing constantly in my mind a saying Mother had used: "It's a poor hen that can't scratch for one chick." Having provided for seven children by working hard at a variety of jobs, Mother didn't have much patience with any woman who couldn't provide for only one child. She would mutter in disgust when looking at those who were in obvious need but not obviously doing anything about it. Mother could be witheringly sarcastic (another pattern that I learned and repeated), and she did not withhold her opinions about those who did not care for their children's needs. So I found myself feeling not only alone and vulnerable but guilty. Like the widow Isaiah spoke to, I felt disgraced by my situation. I should have been able to make my marriage work, but if I chose to divorce, I certainly should be able to provide for us. And because I felt ashamed, I could not tell anyone just how serious my situation was. Having worked my way through college, I had become creative in getting by on almost no money. I had perfected reducing my wants and scrimping on my needs. But my budget clearly showed that without the job I had just lost, I would need $100 more each month than I had coming in.

As I worked at home one day, the phone rang. It was Corrine, one of the women in our small group from church.

"How are you doing?" she asked.

"I'm well, thanks."

"I don't mean your health. I mean, how are YOU doing? How are you coping with all this?"

I assured her that though it was difficult, I was coping pretty well with the pain and loss. She asked if Spencer and I were progressing toward getting the decree granted, and I brought her up to date on the legal maneuvering. Then she asked, "What about money? Are you okay?"

"I'm managing. It's tight, but I'm managing."

"Let me ask this another way: If you or Emily got sick, could you go to the doctor and get prescriptions filled without having to worry about the money?"

"No, I have to say I could not."

"I thought so. I don't want you to have to choose between taking care of yourself and paying the bills. I'm putting a check in the mail." And she did, making it clear that this was a gift, not a loan. She said, "God has blessed us, and giving this is not a hardship. We have it, you need it, and God wants you to take it." The money was a life saver. Or maybe I should say it felt like a lifeline. Instead of feeling like I was alone at sea, struggling to hang on and in danger of going under, I felt like someone was pulling me to safety. I was not alone. Someone was keeping an eye on me. For that month, I was able to pay the bills and to know that if Emily got sick, I could take her to the doctor. It also enabled me to sleep at night.

But the next month, I found myself in the same situation—$100 short of what I needed. Again I found myself feeling scared and alone, worrying and fretting. And again one afternoon as I worked at home, the phone rang. It was a friend who was editor of a magazine. I had written for her many times over the preceding few years. She said. "A feature for the next issue fell through, and I'm in a jam. I need someone to write something, and I need it immediately." Her deadline was only days away. "I know this is short notice," she said, "but can you help me out?" We talked about what she needed, and I told her I'd give it a try. Because of the time crunch, she paid me more than our usual rate. The payment? $100.

Several weeks later, I went to our Wednesday night supper at church. It was followed by the pastor's Bible study, and we often had more than two hundred people around tables in the fellowship hall. I got Emily settled in the nursery and hurried down to the serving line to get my food. I had rushed from teaching my last class to pick up Emmy and get there before they stopped serving, and I was a bit rattled and breathless. As I laughed and talked with another latecomer in line, Helen turned to say, "There you are! We wondered if you were going to make it." She and her husband were also in the small prayer group that Corrine and I were part of. She stepped back and whispered, "Willis and I want you to have this. Just think of it as a little Christmas present." She inconspicuously handed me a folded check. I slipped it into my pocket without even looking at it, giving her a hug and saying thanks. I resumed my conversation. When I got home a few hours later, as I emptied my pockets I pulled out the check. I assumed it would be $20 or so. It was a check for $100. I was beginning to see a pattern.

The second month following that, short of what I needed as usual, I came home one afternoon to find a plain envelope in the mailbox along with my mail. Inside it were five $20 bills. There was no note, nothing. To this day I do not know who placed the money there, but I know who sent it. God sent it.

Month after month until I finished graduate school and got a full-time job, God sent what we needed. It didn't always come in a lump sum as it had these months, but it always came. Gradually, I came to believe that God had taken notice of my situation. I kind of think that the Widow of

Zarephath didn't automatically believe after that first day that the oil and meal would last. Human nature being what it is, I think that for many of those first nights she probably wondered as she fell asleep if the miracle would happen again tomorrow, if the oil and meal would be multiplied. I know I wondered if God would continue providing. Every month, particularly those first months, I would experience the fear, almost panic, each time I faced a need that I had no money for. And every month, God would send someone who would say by words or actions, "God knows. God cares. God will help."

It's lack of faith at worst, poor memory at best that allows us in hard times to forget that God has promised never to leave us. Even the people we love and trust most may leave us, but God never will. God very graciously kept telling me and showing me that I was loved and that I was not alone. One after another, Elijahs came to say to me, "Okay, tomorrow you can give up. But just for today, go ahead and cook the meals. Do what you need to do, and I'll be here with you." It took a long time for me to learn to trust that God would provide day by day.

When the water pump on my car went out, the father of one of my students heard about the situation and insisted on paying for the repairs. I don't know why; he didn't know me. But he said he felt that God wanted him to help out, and he tried to be obedient to those nudgings.

Over and over, things like that happened. Once I allowed a friend to take my car on a long trip. She drove it without checking the oil, and when I got it back, the oil was so low it didn't show on the dipstick. A few months later, the engine blew. I had been trying to save some money, and I had a little, but replacing the engine cost a thousand dollars. That cleaned me out, so much so that I couldn't even pay my utility bills. Dan and Ruth, a married couple we had been friends with for several years, came by my house. Dan asked me how I was coping financially after having to replace the car's engine. I told him I was managing. Then he said, "Do you have enough money to last you till the end of the month?"

"Of course not."

"I thought so," he said. He pulled out his checkbook and wrote me a check for $250. Handing it to me, he said, "I want you to consider this a gift. All I ask is that sometime when you see someone in need and are able to, you pass this along." And so it went, month after month and eventually year after year.

You'd think that after experiences like these I would never worry about whether my needs will be met. Since I am forgetful, however, God graciously continues to send me reminders that I need to learn to lean—though sometimes those reminders look remarkably like unmet needs. One night during the time I was working on this manuscript, I was praying as I walked my dog. (I pray a lot while I walk my dog.) I had just faced a huge car repair bill, and I had virtually emptied my checking account to pay it. Money was tight. I was tempted to worry, and as I became aware of my anxiety, I felt myself grinning as I remembered the events I've written about in this chapter. I said out loud, almost laughingly, "Okay, God, I'm waiting to see how you're going to provide for me until next payday." As I rounded the block and came to my mailbox, I opened it to find a check. It was a refund on homeowners' insurance. I had long since forgotten that it was even coming—but it came, at just the time I needed it.

Years ago, Emily's godfather was struggling to find money for doctoral work in Scotland. Coming from the United States, he had to demonstrate before leaving the states that he had money to pay his expenses and would not need to work while he was in Scotland as a student. The deadline for sending the proof of his self-sufficiency was close, and he didn't have the amount of money he needed. As we talked on the phone, I assured him that God would provide it. He agreed half-heartedly, but he also said he was nervous. Soon after, just days before he was to leave, we talked again. I asked if the money had come in. "Just barely, but it's here," he said.

"I told you God would come through."

"Yeah, but this last-minute stuff is nerve-wracking! Somebody should tell God the banks will take the money a little early and hold it for you!" We laughed about it then, and I laugh about it now, but there's an important principle underlying his experience and mine. Somehow, I think we are meant to trust God day by day, even minute by minute. Learning to trust is not a one-time achievement, a skill like learning to ride a bicycle. It's not a goal like earning a college degree or something to add to a resume under Other Skills/Honors/Achievements: "Learned to Trust God, August 1992." Like the manna that came to the Hebrews in the wilderness each day, God's grace comes to us each day. We can't store it up, and we're not meant to.

If I had all I need for years into the future, I would probably be tempted to forget that, at base, it is God who provides all that I have. I treasure my independence so much that I could begin to feel and act self-sufficient. There's a verse in Deuteronomy that says, "It is [God] who gives you power to get wealth"(v. 8:18) and, I would add, everything else. It is God who allows us to get an education, to find a job, to build relationships, to do all that we do. Though I hate to be needy and to feel needy, my needs remind me to turn to God. They are like a tether—a lifeline, if you will—to keep me from drifting away. And I learn over and over again that having God to lean on is a comfort. I need the Lord.

A part of this experience has also been learning to live in the present rather than in the past. The feelings of fear and vulnerability that I experienced so strongly in those first months after my marriage ended were tied very clearly to my childhood. Rationally, I knew that I was not in the imminent danger that had characterized my life when I was young. But that made no difference. The feelings were as real and as strong as they had been twenty years earlier. My heart would race, my breathing would speed up, I would feel the inward quaking. It took me a long time to hear God saying to me, "That was then. This is now. It is not the same." As an adult I had to learn to look at the reality around me, not at the fearful memories that flooded over me. Though I had been alone and vulnerable once, I would consciously remind myself that this was different. I had to let go of the past and learn new ways of thinking about myself and my life.

Instead of living in fear that tomorrow all I love might be gone, I have to turn my eyes to today and see all the good that God has brought and continues to bring into my life. It is still not easy or automatic for me to do this. Philippians 4:19 says that God will supply all our needs "according to his riches in glory in Christ Jesus"; John 10:10 says that Jesus came to give us life, and that abundantly. But instead of a mindset of God's abundance, I lived with a mindset of scarcity. Gently, God helped me to see that many of my assumptions about life and about people were wrong. Life is sometimes difficult, but that does not mean it is dark. God wills only good for us. Sometimes people get in the way of God's goodness being realized in our lives; sometimes some people are deliberately cruel. But God's goodness does reach us, in countless ways, and many people are good and kind and generous. Like the man carried to Jesus by his friends (Mark 2:1-12), I had Christian friends who helped me when I could not help myself. There were people who cared, and they were proof that God would not leave me alone. The loving people who were God's messengers to me were visible, tangible arguments that challenged my fearful assumptions.

So I began to entertain the possibility that I didn't have to be scared of life. With God's help day by day, I could enjoy the good things each day brought. And as I looked for the goodness of life, I saw it more and more. It's sort of like a game that Emily and I played where we looked for Volkswagen "bugs" (Super Beetles, the little cars with the rounded tops) while we were in traffic. I never realized how many there are until we started looking, and then I saw them everywhere. When I look, I see God's grace all around me. It is grace that brings us sunshine and warm weather, grace that brings us a smile from a stranger, grace that gives us a juicy orange or warm cookies and cold milk, grace that provides shelter and friends. To the eye that looks for it, as Elizabeth Barrett Browning put it in one of her poems, "every common bush" [is] "afire with God." God is unfailingly good. Though we may forget to trust God's faithfulness and goodness, God is still faithful.

Every day is filled with reminders of God's grace, and it doesn't trickle into our lives. It floods. This spring I've been noticing the seeds that the maple trees put out. There are thousands of the seeds, literally. Every crevice in my patio is full of them; piles of them blow up against every windbreak, every step. The lawns in my neighborhood are dotted with the little winged things. There are more seeds than we could ever gather. I have come to believe that that's how God's grace is—profligate, extravagant, unrestrained, overwhelming in its richness, coming at us in so many ways that we can never capture or take advantage of it all. God is not into subsistence but abundance, and all that God has is ours. Like butter slathered on a hot roll so it runs over our hands and down our chins, God's grace flows toward us.

Having experienced all of this, most of the time I am able to tell myself convincingly that even if it takes a miracle, God can do what I need. And in those times when I can't convince myself, when I'm almost ready to give in to despair, one of God's messengers comes along to help me learn again that I can lean on the everlasting arms.

CHAPTER 6

A BITTER ROOT

CLEAN WHITE BOXES

I closed a feeling up
in a clean, slick, white box
and put it on a shelf,
then gently closed the closet door.
I held the cool gray keys to all the locks
and hugged them to myself.

Each
time I'd
add a box I'd note
how straight and neat
the stacks were growing as
the feelings mounted up within
my tiny, quiet, safe, and tidy cell.

But one day I made up
an ordinary box—pedestrian, austere—
and when I put it on the shelf,
the whole mess fell
around me—
a heap of old, old feelings
rancid, moldy, bitter,
that had spoiled for being hidden.

Like manna,
feelings do not keep well. [1]

"Have you ever tried to hold one of those inflatable vinyl beach balls under water? It can be done, but it takes both of your hands and all of your attention," said the speaker. "Trying to deny negative feelings and experiences is like trying to hold one of those beach balls under water." As Keith Miller addressed a conference for single adults that I was attending, he went on to talk about the need to face the past and deal with its hurts.

If we try to avoid our sadness, grief, and anger by pushing those feelings down inside, by ignoring them, we are holding down an emotional beach ball. Doing so takes energy and attention. Figuratively speaking, our emotional hands are busy holding down that ball of emotions. If something else comes along that demands our attention, we may be momentarily distracted. When we remove our hands (our attention) from the ball, that allows it to come flying out of the water and perhaps hit some innocent bystander. And daily life has many ways of distracting us from the emotional task of hiding old hurts. The distractions don't even have to be large or particularly personal. When I see someone lose it with a store clerk or come unglued over some minor incident, I find myself thinking, "Ah, a beach ball! What I'm seeing here doesn't justify that strong a reaction. There must be something more beneath the surface."

Carrying around unresolved hurts requires energy. As long as we have to carry them and keep them under control, they drain off emotional and spiritual resources. Instead of having all of our energy available for the new situations that each day brings, we must use some of it to babysit the past. Even worse, old hurts can fester and sour, making us sick at heart and even sick physically. Hebrews 12:15 tells us to beware of the "root of bitterness" that can grow and interfere with our spiritual progress. Old hurts can contaminate present relationships. They can influence and even control our responses to people and events—and we may remain unaware of our reasons for doing what we do and reacting as we do.

But part of God's work in us is to free us from the power of past hurts. We can deflate the beach ball. And it is important that we do so. If we do not bring old hurts into the light of God's healing love, if we do not deal with the underlying issues that have caused our distress, they eventually erupt into the present.

One of the saddest stories in the Bible shows us how this can happen. It's the story of David and his son Absalom (2 Sam. 13–19). The story is a little involved, so you may want to read it for yourself later. Amnon, one of David's sons, "falls in love with" Tamar, a beautiful sister of Absalom, another of David's sons. Amnon tricks Tamar into coming into his quarters, and he rapes her. She begs him not to do this, urging him to ask the king to give her to him honorably. But he is strong and overwhelms her. Then he orders his servant to throw her out into the street. Tamar is disgraced, and when her brother Absalom sees her crying and hurt, he takes her into his home where she remains, "sad and lonely" (2 Sam. 13:20, TEV). Absalom is consumed with hatred for Amnon, and he vows revenge. It takes two years, but Absalom schemes and plans until he finally gets Amnon alone. Then Absalom orders his servants to stab him. David is distraught that Amnon has been killed, but he loves both of his sons and so banishes Absalom instead of having him killed for his crime. David mourns for Amnon, but eventually he also begins to long to see Absalom.

Joab, a captain in David's army and apparently a friend as well, sees how the king longs for his son. Wanting to help David in his sadness, Joab comes up with a plan. He arranges for a woman to come and tell the king a sad story about her two sons, one of whom has killed the other. The woman tells David how the living son has been exiled and cannot return because he would be killed in retaliation for what he did. She asks the king to find a way to allow her remaining son to return; she doesn't want to lose both of them. As David listens to her, he realizes that the story is really about him and his two sons and that losing a second son will not make up for losing the first one to violence.

David asks the woman if Joab has put her up to this. (Perhaps Joab is known for his maneuverings, since David sees Joab's hand in this.) Seeing the lesson, David allows Absalom to return from exile. But the two are not reconciled. In fact, Absalom lives two years in Jerusalem without even seeing his father. Finally Absalom is allowed to come before the king. We might expect a tearful scene of reunion and forgiveness or a hostile confrontation about what happened, but there is no mention of the pain and disgrace and loss that have poisoned their family's life. David and Absalom do not face the issues. So far we have seen four responses to this family's pain and loss: Tamar lives "sad and lonely," consumed by it (2 Sam. 13:20); Absalom strikes and then runs (2 Sam 13:28, 34); David distances himself from it (2 Sam. 14:13); and Joab tries to fix it by manipulating people (2 Sam. 14:2). None of these responses moves them toward reconciliation.

On the contrary, what follows is deepening resentment. Absalom begins secretly to build an army to oppose his father. Eventually Absalom mounts a rebellion, and the fighting begins. But when this happens David seems more concerned about his son than about his kingdom, asking anxiously when a messenger comes from the front, "And the young man Absalom, is it well with him?" (AP). The messenger cannot bring himself to say. A second messenger comes, and the scene is repeated. Both messengers are frightened that the king might have them killed if they bring the bad news that Absalom has fallen in battle. Everyone knows that the king loves his handsome son, and no one wants to tell him what has happened. Finally a young Cushite comes to deliver the message he has been given. When David again asks, "And the young man Absalom, is it well with him?" the young messenger says what he thinks will please the king: "May all your enemies be as he is" (2 Sam. 18:32, AP). In other words, Absalom is dead.

Overwhelmed with grief, David goes to the city walls and cries out. Mourning his losses, David cries out, "O my son Absalom, O Absalom, my son, my son!" (2 Sam. 19:4). Here is a father whose daughter has been deeply wounded, who has lost two sons he loves. Though he has had opportunities, he has never said that he wishes their situation could be different.

And it could have been different. David and Absalom never dealt with the hurt between them, with the deep issues that were tearing their family apart. They were civil to one another, but Absalom's rage at Amnon's misuse of power and at his sister's disgrace was never dealt with; David's grief about Amnon's death and about this beloved son going wrong was never dealt with. The issues of loss, of abuse of power, of the pain of separation were never faced. David's love for his sons and the desire for reconciliation were never voiced. Absalom's rage went underground, erupting finally as literal rebellion against his father. And the chance for healing and reconciliation between them died with Absalom in the battle.

All too often in our relationships, the chance for reconciliation dies in the battle. In divorce, the battle is often fierce. A couple may go into the divorce process with years of unresolved hurt. If we refuse to face the issues that have brought us to where we are, the pain can poison our lives as it did the lives of Tamar, David, and Absalom.

But who wants to face the hurt? As I said in the beginning of this book, I was tired of hurting. Just as I did not want to re-live the painful experiences of my childhood, I did not want to go over the ground of my marriage again. However, God knew that I needed to address the underlying issues. If I did not, my hurt and loss could fester in me as Absalom's did within him, becoming a bitterness that could consume me and those whose lives I touch.

I can understand David and Absalom's resistance. There are many reasons not to face the issues. Talking about problems in our families is like undressing in public. We are ashamed to let people know the awful things that happen, so we keep secrets. David's family, especially Tamar, would be disgraced if people knew about the sexual abuse. Breaking the silence can tear a family apart; that's why much abuse goes unreported and unprosecuted. Absalom had to protect his sister from further hurt, so he could not say anything openly. Though the Bible tells us that David was "very angry" about what happened, Abaslom does not deal openly with the trouble between him and Ammon. And the king does nothing. Absalom may have felt that he had to wait for his father to deal with Amnon's crime. Maybe he wanted David to do something to make up for Tamar's humiliation—but he never told him so. David was a king, busy with the affairs of state. He may have been so busy with his political responsibilities that he had no energy to deal with family problems. And all of them might have been waiting for the right time or the right way to approach the pain.

It is easy to avoid dealing with painful issues in our lives by saying that the time is not right. That allows us to push away (banish) the pain and the persons who have hurt us and to continue to deny that we have been hurt and are still hurting. When is the right time? The right time is whenever we become aware that pain from old wounds is leaking into today, interfering with life. That awareness is God calling to us, asking us if we want to be free and to move forward with our lives. If we do, God offers us a way to do so. It's a process called forgiveness.

Forgiveness is the only way to deal with hurts and get free of them. It sounds simple to do, but forgiving is often a long and wrenching process. It is a process, rather than an event or an act. Even deciding that we ought to forgive can take time. Who wants to forgive someone who has inflicted hurt on them year after year? We may feel that it's not fair to absolve others. But if we merely exile them as David did Absalom, if we only put them out of our mind and do not face the issues between us and them, we remain tied to them emotionally. And what or whom we send into exile doesn't just sit there unchanging any more than Absalom did. During the time he was away, his bitterness and anger apparently increased. He came back not meek and repentant but hostile and rebellious. In the same way, when we send our pain and anger into exile they can intensify and become even more powerful and destructive. The past becomes a bigger and bigger beach ball that is harder and harder to hold down.

But forgiveness? Forgiveness applies to sin, not to pain. Well, our pain is often caused by our own and others' sin. And as a friend said to me, "There's always sin in divorce."

"I don't agree. Divorce is not a sin," I answered.

"That's not what I said. I said, 'There's always sin in divorce.'"

"What do you mean?"

"I mean that we are sinful people, and because we are, we end up getting divorced. We disobey God by doing things we know we should not. That's sin."

After thinking about his words for a while, I had to agree. I did not want to admit that there had been sin in my divorce—at least not on my part. Because of my agreement with Spencer at the time we separated, I had not talked about him and the reasons for the end of our marriage. But even though I had not said bad things about him, I did see myself as the more innocent party. After all, I had worked to save the marriage. I had done my part. So it was difficult for me to recognize and name my sin.

It was not as if one of us had had an affair. I think it actually might have been easier in many ways if that had been true. That's the best reason to get a divorce if you're a Christian. If one person has an affair and the marriage breaks up, the faithful spouse can come out of it smelling like a rose. It is a horribly painful experience for a faithful husband or wife to discover that his or her spouse has been unfaithful. I have seen the devastation this causes people. But people accept it when a marriage breaks up because of infidelity. It is much harder for the church to accept that a marriage where both parties are faithful can still be so horribly painful and destructive that people must get out of it. As hard as it is to consider, it seems to me that people would almost prefer that there be an affair.

In my case, even Spencer wanted to believe that there was someone else. Though Spencer seemed deeply relieved at the time the breakup occurred, once he moved out of the house he began to think there must be another man involved in my decision to end our marriage. He followed me and watched the house. He copied a note left on my door by one of my students and took it to his attorney, asserting that because it was signed only with initials it was a love note from another man. The writer was a girl struggling with college whom I had been helping outside of class. She had come to say good-bye before leaving for break and left a note because I was not at home. Since there was no other man there was no "evidence" other than the note, but Spencer continued for some time to believe there was and to accuse me of it. I was hurt by those accusations. I had been as open with him as I could be about my counseling, and I had told him all I could about my struggle and my unhappiness. I guess it seemed easier to blame an outsider than to admit that our weak relationship had fallen apart of its own weight. Infidelity was not my sin.

So what was my sin? The first sin I identified was arrogance. (Yes, there was more than one.) During the months of our engagement, Spencer and I went for premarital counseling. Our college offered it to all students, as a joint project of the psychology and religion departments and those training to be counselors. We had taken a battery of personality tests and gone to counseling sessions. The counselor advised us not to marry. For many reasons, he said, we faced a difficult future if we did. We chose not to take that advice. We believed that our love for one another was more important than the obvious mis-match in our personalities. We knew more than the trained people who loved us and were trying to help us. In retrospect, I could see that God had tried to save us from the pain we inflicted on one another.

Then there was disobedience and cowardice. I thought of the summer before our wedding. I had been consumed with doubts about whether I should marry Spencer. I had a nagging uneasiness inside that never went away, and I prayed repeatedly asking God to close the doors and to stop our wedding if I was doing the wrong thing. That continual knowing was God's voice, and I chose to disregard it. That is disobedience. I had wanted God to step in front of me and do something rather than ask me to take responsibility for my situation. And I did think about calling off the wedding. But hundreds of invitations had gone out, the arrangements were all made, and I felt I would die of embarrassment if we did not go through with it. That was cowardice and pride. God had given me the guidance I asked for, but I refused to listen. My pride kept me from hearing what God kept saying. Looking back, I could see my sin. I didn't want to see it, but it was there. So I asked God to forgive me for my arrogance and disobedience, my pride, my cowardice and my hardness of heart. I asked God to help me always to listen when the Holy Spirit spoke in my heart about something I had done wrong.

Then I began to be aware of the pain the divorce had caused for Spencer. This was not what I had had in mind. I assumed that the forgiveness thing between me and Spencer had been taken care of when we prayed together before he moved out. But now I felt that I had to ask forgiveness again for hurting Spencer, even though what had hurt him most was my doing what I felt I had to do. So I prayed again for forgiveness.

And then there was his mother. Catherine was the best of what it means to be a Southern lady. She was the soul of kindness and compassion, a wonderful Christian, and a loving mother-in-law. No one could have asked for a warmer welcome into the family than she had shown me. I adored her. The pain she felt at our divorce was clearly visible in her eyes. She was deeply wounded by the thought that her dear son was losing his family, and she feared that I would keep her from Emily. I did not intend to, of course, but she still feared it. She was deeply hurt, and I was partly to blame for that hurt. I needed to let her know how much I regretted it. So I wrote her a long letter, trying to help her understand that I loved her and would never intentionally hurt her or Spencer.

I asked God to forgive me, and I asked the people I had hurt to forgive me. But the need for forgiveness goes in other directions, as well. By acknowledging that I could no longer endure the hurt of being in my marriage, I was admitting that there had been hurt. Being told year after year, over and over, that I was unacceptable in almost every way was cruel. I had to forgive Spencer for that. Being accused of infidelity and called a liar in the legal system was unkind and mean. But acknowledging the hurt and the need for forgiveness was not my first response. My first response was to minimize what had gone on and to pretend that I was not all that deeply wounded. For a while this allowed me to avoid forgiving and to avoid thinking about the things I wanted to forget.

Eventually, though, my hostility caught up with me. One evening as Emmy and our friend Charles and I were finishing dinner, Spencer called to talk about some arrangements for getting Emmy. We had joint custody, and we had to talk often about meeting times and return times. We finished that part of the conversation and went on to other things. Spencer said something, and I quickly became angry. I said something harsh back to him and hung up the phone in exasperation. Charles sat quietly for a while and then said, "I guess you're not really free of him yet, are you?"

"What do you mean?"

"If he can make you that angry that quick, you're not free." Charles was right. I asked God to help me forgive Spencer because I wanted to be free. Forgiving him was the grace God wanted developed in me, and I set about yielding to forgiveness. I prayed about it and I wrote in my journal about it. I wasn't ready to forgive, but I asked God to make me willing to be made willing.

Gradually, I was able to talk with Spencer and keep my emotions under control. I would still feel anger churning in my stomach, but I was determined to be kind and patient. I read somewhere that as long as we become upset inwardly or outwardly about past hurts, we are not truly free of them. I was able to remain calm outwardly long before I achieved calm inwardly. I adopted a sort of detachment, as if he were someone I might meet at church or in the office. I had no particular investment in what he said about me or about other things; his comments were simply his opinions. When he came to pick Emily up for his visits, our interactions became more cordial.

But that alone is not enough, of course. David and Absalom had managed to be cordial, showing us that cordiality can hide a world of pain and anger. I had hidden my pain and anger for years during my marriage, at times even from myself, and I wanted not just to be able to control the expression of it but to have it gone. The old hurts tugged at me, coming to mind often and disturbing my facade of composure and competence. It was as if I could not let go of them. And of course, I had not.

One of the most difficult things for me to understand about human nature is how we cling to our pain. Sometimes it is almost as if it defines who we are. If we let go of it, who will we be? What will draw the outlines of our life? I think about my mother and her painful life. She grew up desperately poor in the hard-scrabble culture of Kentucky coal-mining towns, and life was difficult. Her mother left her and her brother when they were preschoolers and died when Mother was nine years old. While her dad worked in the coal mines, she and her brother lived with relatives who mostly didn't want them.

Mother was never able to let go of the view that the world is a harsh and unfriendly place and that life is mostly struggle. I always wished that she could see the world as a more welcoming place. Maybe she could have been more welcoming toward others if she had. But she could not let go of the great pain she had endured, and she was critical and pessimistic about human nature and about life. Her pain both defined and limited who she was.

If I did let go of the hurts, I would also be shaped and limited by them. The pain had been great, but the hurts Spencer and I had inflicted on each other had not sprung from malice. As his deep needs went unmet and his pain increased, he lashed out at me because I was the one who was there. He did not realize what he was doing. And even when he lashed out in malice, he did not realize how deeply his actions hurt me. I had to forgive him. If I did not, the hurt I carried would sour within me and turn into bitterness.

We do not have to wait for others to change or to ask for forgiveness.

Jesus' example on the cross shows us this. When he prayed, "Father, forgive them; for they know not what they do" (Luke 23:34, KJV), he gave us a model that can transform our way of dealing with those who hurt us. We don't have to wait for them to repent and ask for our forgiveness. That may never happen. But we can forgive them and leave behind what they have done to us. I wanted to forgive, to leave the pain behind for good. I wasn't sure how I would know when I had done this.

As I talked with my counselor and prayed, I came to believe that Spencer was probably in as much pain as I was, maybe even more, and I began to pray for him. During our conversation about my filing for divorce, I had told Spencer I was sorry for hurting him, but I said that with little understanding of his pain. I had not really believed that I had done much. Now I found myself wondering how he felt at losing his home. One of the two things we had going for us, according to our pre-marital counselor, was that we both deeply wanted marriage and a Christian home. Spencer adored Emily, and I began thinking about the pain he must have felt at being separated from her. I found myself praying for him frequently. Many of the prayers were the same ones I had prayed before our divorce, but now I was praying those things for him, not out of the self-interest that had driven me to try to save our marriage. I was able to see and admit the good things about him and to acknowledge the good there had been in our marriage. When I was able to care about him and pray sincerely for God's best for him, then I knew I was truly free of the hurts that had built up over the years.

There remained one more person to forgive: myself. The anger that was so close to the surface of my emotions had not come only because of what Spencer had done. I was also angry at me. I truly wanted to be perfect. Admitting the magnitude of my mistake in marrying made me feel stupid, and I really hate to feel stupid. In my way of looking at the world, other people are permitted to make mistakes, but I am not. I encourage others not to be too hard on themselves, but I have to do it right. Eventually, I came across something that helped me surrender that unattainable standard. Some sort of spiritual exercise led me through considering how I would help a close friend who was facing a struggle (I'm not even sure the struggle was a sin—just some sort of struggle). At the end of the exercise was a question something like, "Do you treat yourself this way when you are going through a struggle?" I saw that if God would want me to deal gently with others, I had to believe God wanted me to deal gently

with myself too. I still remind myself of this strategy often. When I'm flog-
ging myself mentally for something I've done, I stop and say to myself,
"Would you treat your best friend this way?" I think of Frieda, my best
friend, and realize I would try to be gentle and loving with her. Then I am
able to be more loving toward myself.

I believe that God is continually guiding each of us toward forgiveness.
God wants to mend our hearts that have been wounded in hurtful relationships and set us free to love without strings attached. I know that God
has acted that way in my life, and I have come to believe that it is a general
spiritual principle. One of the people who convinced me of that was
Spencer. One cold January afternoon a few years ago as I worked in my
office, the phone rang.

"Mary Lou? This is Spencer."

"Well, hello!"

"Is this a convenient time for you to talk? Do you have a few minutes?"

"Sure. What do you need?"

"Well, I called because I want to ask your forgiveness."

He went on to ask forgiveness specifically for things he had done to
hurt me during our marriage and while we were divorcing. Then he asked
forgiveness for anything he had done in the years since to hurt me, ending
with, "I'm sorry, and I ask you to forgive me if you can." For a few
moments I was speechless (which is pretty rare for me). Finally I recovered
my voice and told him that of course I forgave him, that I had done so
many years earlier.

We talked a bit more, and I said to him, "May I ask why you are doing
this now? I mean, why today? What happened to bring you to do this?" He
had been praying during a prayer vigil at his church, and it occurred to
him that though he had asked God to forgive him, he had never asked me
to—and he felt he needed to do that. It had taken years—many years—after
our divorce for us to come to this place, but I believe it was God's grace that
brought us both here. In a later conversation Spencer told me that the experience was momentous for him. It came at a time in his life when spiritual
change was taking place, and for him to call me was a big thing. He said,
"It was the Lord who was working in me to bring me to that place."

The tension and animosity, the inner uneasiness, are gone. When we
are together for important events in our daughter's life, we can share meals
and laugh about our younger years. I inquire about his life, his family, his

wife and stepchildren. We care about each other and can show care toward each other. I pray for him and his family, and I know he prays for me. We have talked about that.

This doesn't mean that I have never gotten annoyed at Spencer since then. He still does things in his relationship with Emmy that I disagree with. But when I get angry with him, it is about things that are happening now, not things that I've saved up from long ago, and the anger doesn't last long or overwhelm me. In this relationship at least, the hurts of the past no longer contaminate the present.

My path and his in coming to this place have been very different, but I believe that God wants to guide each of us along a road that leads toward forgiveness. We know that not everyone chooses to face the pain they have suffered and inflicted. And sometimes the way is long and winding, especially when the hurts have been deep. But there is a wide, good place at its end. This is a gift of grace.

---

[1]"Clean White Boxes" first appeared in *alive now!* May/June 1982.

CHAPTER 7

"A PEW FOR ONE, PLEASE"[1]

I was having lunch with my friend Rachel, with whom I taught English and played racquetball. We attended the same church, our children played together, and we and our husbands had socialized with other co-workers. Rachel and I had known each other for several years. Her husband was a scientist, an anomaly among all us literary types, and he looked at the world very differently than most of the people I knew. For some time I had been trying to decide if I even liked him, and finally I had come to the conclusion that I did. He always made me think, and that is a valuable kind of person to know. He shook some of my comfortable assumptions, and I value that.

As we ate our lunch on this day as we often had, Rachel began telling me some story about her husband. I took this occasion to say to her, "You know, Rachel, I really like Bruce. For years I've been unsure about whether I like him or not, but I have finally decided that I do. He's a neat guy."

Smiling, she said, "That's nice. Stay away from my husband."

I looked at her in disbelief. "Rachel! We've been friends for years."

Smiling even more broadly, pausing with half a sandwich midway to her mouth, she spoke again. "I know." Then, speaking very slowly and deliberately, looking directly into my eyes, pausing between words, she continued, "And I said, 'Stay . . . away . . . from . . . my . . . husband.'"

That conversation opened my eyes to a set of attitudes I didn't even realize existed. Because I was divorced, my friend felt she now had to warn me away from her husband. We were both Christians, teaching at a Christian college, and she still felt it necessary to make it clear to me that her husband was off limits. I was suddenly no longer trustworthy; I was a divorced woman, and that made me suspect. Never mind that we had known one another for years and that we had sat side by side in worship. All that counted for nothing because I had gotten a divorce.

But she wasn't the only one. When I called to have the lease on our house changed from mine and my husband's name jointly to my name alone, the property manager said, "Well, I'm not sure we can do that. We don't usually rent to divorced people."

"Excuse me?"

After stumbling around some phrases about policy, he said, "Well, I suppose if you don't play music too loud or disturb the neighbors or have parties. . . . I'll have to talk to some people here." (The house adjoined a complex of a religious organization, and the organization had bought it and several other houses along the street for possible future expansion.)

"So you're saying that I have to behave because I live in your house? And I have to behave because of where I teach—Gosh, I guess I'll just have to turn over a whole new leaf and clean up my act!"

Realizing that I was disturbed, the man said, "I didn't mean it that way. It's just that we don't usually rent to single people. I'll look into it and let you know if we can renew the lease in your name alone."

"Well, should I just have my attorney call you? He's helping me with the other stuff."

After a pause he cleared his throat and said, "Oh, since you've been in the house for a while, we can probably work something out. I'll call you back."

The most arresting thing about these conversations was that all the people involved were Christians. I was naive, I suppose, but I thought that people who knew me would continue to see me as me. I was sad and emotionally fragile, but I was still the same person I had always been.

There were other less blatant clues that my status had changed. Someone at church asked me which Sunday school class I was going to be attending. Spencer and I had been part of a couples class for several years by this time, and I had not considered that I would have to leave the class. Of course it was not officially required—but it was also expected that I would not be staying in the class. These were the people with whom my husband and I had socialized, done mission outreach, prayed, and studied the Bible. That didn't matter. Once I was no longer part of a couple, I was expected to leave the group.

At a time when I needed love and support, I was finding out that in many ways, I stood alone. Many of our friends expressed their concern for both of us, but a single person in couples settings made the numbers odd—and ultimately, made me feel odd.

Even within the church staff, I was something of a problem. Take the case of Darlene. She is a compassionate, caring person, and I felt close to her. One day we met outside the church office as she hurried to a meeting, arms laden with schedules and materials to distribute.

"How are you doing?" she asked in her kind, concerned way.

"I'm doing all right, I guess."

"I know this is a hard time for you," she said tenderly. "I just wish I had time to minister to you."

We both burst out laughing at the irony of her words. We served on the church staff together. She was in charge of our church's caring ministry, organizing people to help when there was a special need. She also coordinated our extensive prayer ministry. The irony of what she had said was clear to both of us. Her job was to care for people—but she was too busy doing that to have time for me. We were friends as well as co-workers, and I knew she was truly concerned about me and the struggle I was going through. That made no difference. Our regular way of interacting did not provide an opportunity for her to give me any special attention—and I understood.

For most of us with our full lives, taking time to help those who are in some kind of crisis requires that we put aside something else. What should I ask or expect Darlene to give up? Calling prayer groups to pass on the names of those with urgent needs? Training volunteers? Studying with other leaders? Caring for her own family? None of these, of course. What she was doing was worthwhile. It was God's work, and I knew that she felt a genuine calling to do what she was doing.

I couldn't judge her because I was very much like her. Until my own divorce, I did not notice or reach out to those around me who were divorcing. I remember our prayer group praying for people at various times, but I do not recall ever having a serious conversation with someone whose marriage was ending. I'm sure I must have had contact with people in the midst of divorce—but their needs had not seemed pressing enough that I took time to comfort them or to listen to them.

Her response to me, my past responses to others (or rather, the lack thereof), and the responses of others in the church remind me of the parable of the Good Samaritan. In this parable, the man who had been beaten by robbers and left on the road was in need of care. Some might have considered him at least partly to blame for his situation; he could have been called unwise for taking that road alone, leaving himself vulnerable. If he had been more careful, the robbery and beating might never have happened. Nevertheless, he was in need. He was in pain, and he was vulnerable.

Like that man, if I had been wiser and more obedient, I might have avoided the pain. I might not have entered a damaging marriage that left me wounded and unable to function much of the time. But you cannot unscramble eggs, and I could not undo what I had done. Perhaps the situation was of my own making, but the pain was still overwhelming, and I needed help that I could not give myself. I didn't even know what I needed. I just knew that I hurt.

In the parable, the priest and the Levite both passed by on the other side of the road, avoiding the man who had been beaten. There are various explanations, even good reasons, for their doing what they did. The Bible story says the beaten man was "half dead" (Luke 10:30, TEV). The priest may have thought the man was completely dead. Touching a dead person would make him ritually unclean, and he would not have been able to carry out his priestly duties. Perhaps he was on his way to the Temple; perhaps this was his one time in the year to go into the Holy of Holies, to approach God on behalf of the people. He might have been the one chosen. There was a service about to begin, and maybe he was the celebrant. Or maybe he feared that the robbers were still lurking nearby, ready to pounce on him. Maybe he even thought the man lying on the ground was a decoy, part of a trap to get him to stop so that he could be robbed. Whatever the case, the priest—the minister—passed by on the other side of the road.

There are several parallels between my supposings about the priest in the parable and clergy in our churches today. In dealing with divorced people, clergy sometimes have to walk a thin line between ministry to them and supporting marriage and the traditional family. The accepted pattern in our culture is marriage, especially in the church, and commitment to a partner is praiseworthy. Last spring I noticed a letter to the editor in a news magazine praising Howard Stern, the often offensive radio talk-show host. He does not get much public praise for his support of traditional values. The writer noted that Stern has "stayed with his first and only wife through thick and thin, which is more than can be said for moral 'conservatives' such as Bob Dole, Ronald Reagan, Newt Gingrich and Phil Gramm."[2]

Publicly supporting ministry to people like me may be seen as an endorsement of divorce. People who divorce are open to criticism. The criticism may come, in fact, almost automatically. During the presidential campaign in 1996, CNN reporter Susan Rook had to apologize publicly for a comment she made about Bob Dole. A representative of the Republican National Committee was extolling Dole's virtues and said,

"When he gives you his word, you can take it to the bank."

"Which word are we talking about?" asked Rook. "The word to his first wife when he said 'Until death do us part?' "[3]

We don't want to seem too easy on people who divorce. That can make it difficult for clergy who encounter hurting people and want to help. And even if a pastor cares and wants to reach out, there are always attitudes like my friend Rachel's. Male pastors must be circumspect with single women, and female pastors must be the same with single men. Divorced people are suspect, and pastors may feel that they have to protect themselves by steering clear of close involvement. I can see why clergy sometimes feel they have to pass by on the other side of the road and not get involved.

The Levite also passed by the beaten man. Levites were from the tribe of Levi, those who traditionally cared for the Temple. They served God and were supported by the tithes given them by the people. They are like paid people who work for the church but are not ordained—sort of like my friend Darlene, or the church secretary, the administrator, the building superintendent. Or like me. All of us on our church staff believed in what we were doing. We had over a dozen full-time church staff, and every one of us worked hard. Most church staff are already overworked, and asking them to pay attention to another special group—this time, the divorced people—is asking a lot. They are already pulled between the children's program, the youth program, the marriage enrichment programs, the family ministry programs, the music program; the stewardship campaign; finding church school teachers; overseeing the child-care center, mission outreaches, the clothing closet, and the food bank—each one of them a worthwhile ministry that needs to be done, with more causes waiting for a champion to take them on. Church staff are already too busy.

Many professional caregivers—and even the general public—are sometimes described these days as suffering from "compassion fatigue." Compassion fatigue is what it sounds like—being tired of caring. Caregivers such as counselors, relief workers, medical personnel, and those who work for the church give of themselves constantly, without a vacation from taking care of others. Eventually they may begin to feel that they cannot care for even one more person. There is constant pressure to learn the newest information about emerging new syndromes, to care about new groups of people. Caregivers are often so busy learning and caring for others that they have little time for themselves. New areas of expertise emerge all the time, and there are still only twenty-four hours in each day. How can they take time to reach out to yet another group of needy people? I was one of those busy church staff people, and I knew how busy the others were.

Turning aside to take care of those who are wounded takes time, energy, and personal investment that people sometimes simply cannot give. I understood that. When I laughed with Darlene in the hall outside the church office that day, I knew the impossible position people sometimes find themselves in. I could not blame the church staffers for going on with their responsibilities. There were people waiting for them, whole groups of people, not just one individual like me. Like the Levite who had to get to the Temple to prepare for the services, they had to take care of their jobs. People were counting on them.

And then there were people like Rachel, people who were simply afraid of me. Divorce can be frightening. When I told one of my Christian friends about my impending divorce, she said, "No! Not you! You've got your head on straight. If this could happen to you, why, it could happen to anybody. It could even happen to me!" Divorce makes people worry about their own marriages. I've heard people talk about "gay divorcees" and worry that divorce seems almost contagious. People seem afraid that if husbands and wives get too close to divorced people, that might put ideas in their heads.

I was not imagining the attitudes that some Christians have toward divorced people; I had expressed those attitudes myself. Early in my marriage, our friend Margaret told us about a new guy she was dating. I liked everything she told us about him. But when I found out that he was in his later twenties—an "older man" for a college woman—I asked if he was divorced. When Margaret said he was, I urged her not to date him any more. She said, "But we're just going out. It's not like I'm planning to marry him or anything."

"But what if you fall in love? What will you do then?" I had not met this man, but without even knowing him I was writing him off as a bad risk, as trouble, as not good for Margaret, simply because he was divorced. That one piece of information was enough for me to know how to evaluate him. That's called prejudice—pre-judging a person. When I met him and got to know him, I liked him immensely and thought all the good things Margaret had said about him were true. But that did not outweigh the fact that he was divorced. I knew the attitudes of many of the people around me toward divorced people—and now I was in that category.

Whether I was sensing what others actually thought or simply projecting my own uneasiness onto them, I felt like a pariah. I felt as if people were veering around me in the halls of the church.

Doing anything at church, attending any program alone, was difficult, but attending worship alone was the worst. I felt as if every eye in the sanctuary were on me. I would pause in the entry hall, wondering where to sit and with whom. If I sat where Spence and I had always sat, his absence was obvious to me and to others. If I sat in a new place, alone, I felt lonely. Each time I came in, I had to face the reality of my new status. Should I sit where Spence and I usually sat together? I couldn't do that without crying. But sitting anywhere else felt strange too. When I looked around, I could see only couples. I couldn't find any place that seemed right.

Many divorced people do exactly what I considered—they turn around and walk out of the church. They can't make themselves go in. They turn and leave—and many don't come back for a very long time, if at all. Some go to other churches, if they can find one where they feel comfortable. Some go back to a former church, perhaps to one their parents or other family members attend. Some simply cannot sit in worship alone and so ask a friend to attend church with them for a while. I tried a variety of strategies. Sometimes I sat with a couple or an individual from our small group. Sometimes I sat alone in one of the small alcoves at the side of the church, trying to be invisible. Sometimes I just didn't go to worship.

One thing that complicated matters a bit was that Spence and I both continued to attend our church. We encountered one another in the halls from time to time, but there was no great animosity between us, so that was not a major problem. I think others were more uncomfortable about both of us being there than Spence and I were. We both participated in many programs of the church, and neither of us wanted to lose the friendships and the familiarity that make a church feel like home. However, in smaller congregations, one partner may feel forced to leave in order to avoid contact with the other, which means that divorcing people often lose their "church home" as well as their legal one.

When you're hurting inside as much as I was hurting, being in church can make the pain even more intense. I felt my failure all the more acutely when I was around people I knew disagreed with what I had done. Spence and I had agreed not to talk about each other, and so people had no information beyond that we had split up. They could not understand our decision, and more painful to me than that, they assumed we had made it lightly. Have you heard comments like, "People just aren't committed to marriage anymore," or, "Well, everyone has rough times, but that doesn't mean you give up and walk out"? I heard them a lot. And they're still being made.

Barbara D. DaFoe Whitehead is author of a new book called *The Divorce Culture: How Divorce Became an Entitlement and How It Is Blighting the Lives of Our Children.* Whitehead does not want to ban divorce completely, but she believes people divorce too easily. She spoke to a reporter about young adults' attitudes. "They're generous and accepting about their own parents' divorce, but they want to put a lot of work into their marriages."[4] This implies that those who are divorced have not "put a lot of work" into their marriages. She believes our "consumeristic values" feed the divorce rate by teaching people "If you don't like what you have, you can trade it in"[5]—including a spouse. She's not the only one who thinks like this.

A close friend I met after my divorce held strong opinions about marriage and divorce. One day after we had known each other for several years, something came up in conversation about my marriage. She asked casually, "How long were you and Spencer married, anyway?"

"Seven years."

"Really! I guess you did give it a fair chance, then, didn't you?" She will never know how much those words hurt me. How could she know me as well as she did and assume that I gave up on my marriage without giving it "a fair chance"? Ending my marriage was a wrenching decision that I made after working hard for years trying to salvage the relationship. And, Mrs. Whitehead's and my friend's comments notwithstanding, I don't think I am unusual in that regard. In all the years I've worked with single people in the church, I have never met anyone who took divorce lightly, who gave up on a marriage because someone left the cap off the toothpaste or wore the wrong fragrance. Divorce is serious, painful, and a last resort.

Getting a divorce is an admission of failure of a relationship, and in a society that's as enamored of success as ours is, failure of any sort is bad for one's resume. In some corporations, an ostensibly happy family is requisite for advancement. Being a "solid, family person" is a career asset (provided your family doesn't require your time and attention in a way that interferes with the job). It's that way in the church too, though we are hesitant to admit it. When I was being considered for one church job, those conducting the search called someone who knew someone who called someone in another organization I had worked for. Those doing the hiring wanted to know confidentially if, since I was divorced, I was "stable." The person they asked assured them I was—and immediately called me to tell me about the inquiry. I laughed about it, since I felt sure I was quite stable. But that question reveals the kinds of assumptions about divorced people that add to the pain. I have deliberately not said much about the specifics of the problems in my marriage. I made that choice partly to guard my former husband's privacy as much as I could and partly because what the problems were doesn't matter. Every marriage has its own problems, and bad marriages have an infinite array of destructive and painful ones. Wanting to know the gory details is voyeurism, in my opinion. Suffice it to say that people who come to the decision to end a marriage do so because they feel there is no other option they can live with. I did what I had to do. Though I needed people to understand that, the church was uncomfortable, and I was uncomforted.

But back to the story of the Good Samaritan. The wounded man left bleeding on the roadside was not left there indefinitely. Eventually someone came along who responded to him—a Samaritan, not someone well thought of in those parts. I like to think that this Samaritan was moved by compassion because he knew what it was like to be alone and to have no one care. He knew what it was to be an outsider, even an outcast, to have people cross the street to avoid contact with him. And when he saw the beaten man, he took time to kneel beside him and dress his wounds. He picked him up, took him to an inn, and arranged for the innkeeper to care for the man.

The people who turned aside to help me, who took time to notice that I was in pain, were other single adults. Some of my good Samaritans were divorced; some had always been single. But each understood what it was like to be alone. They saw that I was bleeding emotionally, and they were willing to get involved. It was not as if they had answers; they were hurting as much as I was. In fact, we took turns taking care of one another. In this group, I was able to cry, to mourn my loss. In other settings I had to hold it together and take care of what had to be taken care of. I couldn't cry at work, even though I often wanted to. But with these people I could cry. Someone would put an arm around my shoulder and just let me cry. Or someone would simply hand me tissues. No one told me not to be upset or that everything was going to be all right. They just let me slog along through the grief, holding my hand.

These people were what Henri Nouwen calls "wounded healers," those who are able to help others because they have suffered pain. These people embodied that concept. We all had our pain and loss to deal with, but that didn't mean we couldn't help one another. I came to realize that God has always used imperfect people, there being no other kind available. In fact, our greatest losses and brokenness often become our door to helping others.

It's not our successes and strengths that help us to learn compassion, that help us learn to "feel with" others. It is our failure, loss, and pain—our wounds—that teach us how others feel, that soften our hearts. We are all wounded in some way, and God can use that. God used that group of single Samaritans to help me make a new place for myself in the church. They became the ones I sat with, the ones who called if I was absent, the ones who came and took care of Emily when I was sick. We named our Sunday school class *Maranatha!* In the early church, this was an affirmation about Jesus' return, a part of prayer that meant, "Come, Lord Jesus." For us, it was a way of saying that Christ was among us. We experienced Christ's presence in one another.

The church was a bit wary of us, just as we were wary of the "older" single adults. The singles group met not in the church but in a basement room of an adjoining building. (That basement room was called, some said symbolically, the "Sarcophagus." A sarcophagus is the container or stone coffin a mummy is buried in.) The physical separation mirrored the feeling that I often thought the larger church had toward us on many levels.

When I think about the Good Samaritan, I am grateful for whatever it was that made him the caring man he was. We aren't told much about him in the Bible story. We don't know what business he was in, whether he had a family, what had happened that caused him to stop that day. We don't know if he had been beaten himself in the past, whether he was part of a family that cared for a chronically ill member. We don't know what experiences made him a person of compassion. Whether it was an experience of pain, loss, helplessness, or vulnerability, it engendered in him the quality for which he is most remembered. He is the "good" Samaritan, the one who cared.

Over the years since my divorce, my primary place of ministry in the church has been with single people. I have done many other things in the church, but singles ministry has been my constant involvement, the thing I keep coming back to, the ministry of the church to which I have given the most hours. The greatest failure in my life has become the primary door to ministry. I've seen something similar happen in other people's lives. Their greatest loss or greatest trial has become their door to ministry. For some, it has been the death of a child. For others, it has been the loss of a career or some serious illness. In the aftermath of the pain, these people find a way to use it. The deeper understanding of others' pain and the compassion we learn makes us able to listen and to care for people we never even noticed before. Our heartache, our great loss, can be transformed into healing for ourselves and for others. It allows us to become wounded healers.

---

[1]The title of this chapter is not original with me. It's the title of a book about singles in the church published in the 1970s.

[2]"News and Views," *USA Weekend* (April 25-25, 1997): 5.

[3]*USA Today* (October 18, 1996): 9A.

[4]Interview by Ray Waddle, "Writer Takes on Divorce," *The Tennessean* (Sunday, March 16, 1997): 1B.

[5]Ibid.

CHAPTER 8

"I AM YOUR FAIRY GODMOTHER"

When you were a kid, did you play "dress up"? I have some great pictures of Emily wearing my high heels and wide-brimmed, southern belle straw hat. The ribbon on the hat flows not down her back but across her chest, and she is holding Toby, our longsuffering white poodle, so he also faces the camera. I love to look at those pictures. I always laugh at the incongruities. Emily has on one of my frilly nightgowns over her flannel pajamas, and her feet fill only the front third or so of my shoes. Toby wears a resigned expression, along with one of Emily's dolls' dresses. It's easy for me to see that those costumes don't fit either of them. Why, then, was it so difficult for me to see that I had been playing emotional "dress up" for most of my life?

When my marriage ended, I didn't know who I was. If I were not Spence's wife, who was I? Who was I going to be? I am amazed at how little thought I had given to answering those questions. I had spent virtually all of my life trying to live up to others' ideals without examining whether those ideals were God's ideals for me and right for me.

Our culture makes it tough for us to form a unique self-image and to value ourselves as we are. Images from advertising, television, and movies come at us, telling us what we ought to be, how we ought to think and feel, how we ought to behave, and how we ought to look.

Some of the most powerful and life-shaping images come from our families. Most of us can complete sentences that begin, "The Isons (fill in one of your family surnames) have always believed in hard work and getting a good education" (fill in your family's favorite expectations), or, "We've had teachers in every generation of this family for over fifty years" (fill in the traditional occupation for someone in your family). How many times have you heard a relative say something like, "That Davidson (or whoever's) stubbornness is going to get you into trouble someday," or, "He's just like his Uncle James"? These comments become like scripts that tell us what is expected behavior, and we hear them in our minds when we are in situations that echo the past.

Other strong images come from our schooling and from the church. Unfortunately, many of the most influential images are media images that repeat relentlessly and in many forms. For me, and I think for most of us, one of the most compelling and distorting of these is the ideal of physical attractiveness.

From the beauty pageants I watched as a child to the current fad of bodybuilding for both men and women, we are bombarded with the message that beautiful is good and that staying young-looking is important. The "cosmetic" surgery industry (where we spent $775 million in 1992)[1] tells women to increase or decrease the size of their breasts and tells both men and women to get nose or eyes "done" or tummy tucked or face lifted as they age. (Did you hear the one about the older woman who's had so many face lifts that her navel is now just below her chin?) I read a review of a book by a local author entitled *Welcome to Your Face Lift* by Helen Bransford. Publishers market books because they feel there are large numbers of people who will buy them, so there must be a lot of people getting facelifts or considering them. (The book tells readers what they can realistically expect, according to the review. But how realistic is it to believe we can cheat time and the force of gravity?) My Sunday newspaper had an article recently about "body sculpting," the practice of liposuction to shape particular body parts. And some super models go so far as to have a rib removed surgically to create a slimmer torso.

The ideal of physical beauty can be a tyrant. When we feel bad about our physical appearance, all our other accomplishments can fade in significance, no matter how noteworthy they may be. A few years ago I read an interview with Dolly Parton. Ms. Parton is an astute businesswoman, a talented writer, and a charismatic stage presence. She has built a multi-million-dollar empire and has helped to revitalize the economy of her home county and surrounding counties in East Tennessee. She is an award-winning performer with a huge following of fans and a philanthropist who cares deeply about people. When the interviewer asked Ms. Parton to name the accomplishment of which she was most proud, Ms. Parton named getting her weight under control.[2] A millionaire businesswoman, and the accomplishment that is foremost in her mind is losing weight! This says volumes about how pervasive cultural ideals can be.

Studies show that attractive people are hired and promoted more quickly than less attractive employees in most organizations. Attractiveness is just another aid to success. An advertisement for a business seminar in *The Tennessean* included various endorsement blurbs, one of which said, "You can never be rich enough or thin enough or successful enough."[3] Business and psychology magazines in recent years have included articles about discrimination against people who are overweight, who have disfiguring birthmarks, or whose appearance has been altered by accidents such as severe burns.

We want everyone, especially the people close to us, to meet certain standards of attractiveness. The horrible phenomenon of eating disorders that take young people's lives is grim proof of just how far some people are willing to go to conform. The same day's newspaper that contained the quote about never being thin enough also carried a story about the death of Heidi Guenther, a talented and promising young ballerina. She died because of anorexia nervosa. Another young dancer who was five feet tall and used to weigh eighty-seven pounds was quoted in the article. She talked about the pressure on dancers to remain not just thin but superthin. When her weight soared to ninety-two pounds, she was put on probation by the dance company and told to lose weight. She said at one point, "If I don't lose eight pounds, I'll get fired."[4] One of the co-authors of the *New Teenage Body Book* estimates that one in 100 young women between the ages of seventeen and twenty-five suffers from anorexia nervosa. Bulimia, the binge/purge eating disorder, affects about four of every 100 young women in that age group.[5] These illnesses have their roots in our cultural attitudes about our appearance. A specialist in eating disorders and author of *Your Dieting Daughter: Is She Dying for Attention?* calls the problem an epidemic.[6] Though media attention to the problem makes it seem a recent phenomenon, years ago daughter of singer and actor Pat Boone wrote *Starving for Love*, a book about her struggle with this deadly disease. Most of those affected by these diseases are females. We are taught that we must be beautiful and that beauty has it rewards. An ad for a diet aid that I saw recently carried a testimonial from a user of the product. She said that her daughter told her she was fat. She began immediately using this product and lost weight. Her daughter now tells her how beautiful she is and, she says, "Life is good." If we can just make ourselves beautiful, life will be good.

I did not examine the cultural forces behind the ideal of beauty; I wasn't even aware that I was being influenced by them. I just wanted to feel and to be physically attractive. My struggle did not begin during my marriage. It goes back to my childhood. In my family, I was repeatedly called "the chubby one." My bedroom was the last one at the end of the hall, and I can remember my brothers whistling "Baby Elephant Walk" as I came down the hall toward the living room. Those experiences shaped my perception of myself.

I am not the only one with such memories. I read recently in the magazine *Walking* about a woman's recollection of something similar from her childhood. The article was a report on her visit to a "fat farm," a program to help people lose weight and change their eating habits. As a youngster, the writer had been playing outside with her brother and a cousin. As they ran from her, they began chanting, "Little Lotta's going to get us! She's going to sit on us!" The writer said that in that moment her image of herself changed. She saw herself suddenly as being like the comic character Little Lotta, an enormously fat child.[7] As an adult, that writer still struggles with her weight. She sees a direct connection between her childhood experience and her continuing problems controlling her weight as an adult.

Like her and many others, I have struggled for years with my weight. When I was in high school, I reached my lifetime heaviest weight of just under 200 pounds. Since I am only 5'2", I was clinically obese. During college I trimmed down and began an exercise program that kept my weight where it should be. But in the year following our wedding, I gained about twenty-five or thirty pounds. Spence gained even more. After he told me the next year that he did not love me, I began dieting. It is not a huge stretch to say that I probably assumed my physical unattractiveness was keeping him from loving me. I dieted and dieted, eventually reaching a weight that I now know was too thin for me. But even when I was at that weight, Spencer urged me to lose ten or fifteen more pounds. And in the aftermath of the dieting, I developed chronic health problems that continued for years.

I wish I could say that my Christian friends helped me to see that what I was doing was dangerous, but that is not true. On the contrary, I saw people take cultural norms about physical attractiveness and thinness and dress them up as theology. Christian small-group programs and books about dieting (though they usually call their plan something like "caring for God's temple" or "stewardship of your body") have been enormously popular. In this country we see being overweight as a character flaw, but in Christian circles it is even worse. Being overweight can become if not a sin at least an area where we need to "practice better discipleship." These attitudes load guilt on top of our already negative feelings about our appearance. And I bought into all of it. I did not accept myself as I was physically.

Then there is my personality. I am very outspoken. Some people call me blunt, even abrupt. After I gave up the manipulative ways of dealing with people that I wrote about earlier, I had no fall-back skills or methods. Once I no longer tried to figure out what people wanted to hear in order to say that, the only thing left to say was what I thought. Some people have difficulty with women who speak their minds. A lot of people have difficulty with women like that. Once in a business meeting at a Christian organization where I worked, I engaged in a spirited debate with a man about some issue we were considering. After the meeting, one of the men said to me, "Doesn't the Bible say women are to be submissive?"

Without even thinking I replied, "It says that women are to submit to their husbands. You may not have noticed it, but I am not married to any of the men who were in that room." Some people have trouble with that sort of directness. I was counseled more than once (usually by male superiors) to be quieter and more subtle in the way I expressed myself. And to be honest, I have often wished I were sweet, gentle, and quiet. I have tried to remind myself to be so, especially in groups. I admire women who seem to be demure, soft-spoken, and gentle by nature.

There are many such ideals that I tried hard to live up to, including being a good wife. I didn't consider doing otherwise because normal people grow up and get married. Comments such as "She's such a nice girl. I wonder why she has never married" or "He's seems like a fine person. Why hasn't he found the right girl and settled down?" spring from the unexamined assumption that people eventually marry unless there is something wrong with them. I had adopted this ideal just as I had all the others, never questioning whether it was right for me.

At first I felt lost after my marriage ended. I felt sort of like Ellen in the movie *Forget Paris*. Ellen (portrayed by Debra Winger) tells her friend Lucy that she doesn't even know "who I am, by myself." Ellen struggles to figure out who she truly is. "I know I'm in here somewhere. I can hear myself screaming from a distance." But I wasn't even that far along in my thinking. I didn't have a clear sense of my own voice because I wasn't even sure a woman alone is supposed to have a voice. I had never thought about my identity apart from marriage; I had not intended to live as a single person.

I was frightened. I felt ugly, incompetent, and condemned. (Someone actually said to me that I had made my bed and now would have to lie in it.) I worried about making it on my own. I felt unsure about whether I could handle life and overwhelmed with responsibility for Emily. And I didn't know how to do many of the things that people have to do to get through life. Day after day, I faced one new challenge after another. I did what I had to do, usually with fear and trembling.

And I began searching in order to find out what God was saying to me. I read books, lots and lots books—about divorce and grief, relationships, family dynamics, self-image. I wrote pages and pages in my journal almost daily. I attended divorce recovery seminars and singles conferences. I read the Bible and talked with other singles and prayed. I read books about women and their struggles, books such as *Speech, Silence, Action* by Virginia R. Mollenkott and *Women, Men and the Bible* by Mollenkott. I read *Heirs Together: Applying the Biblical Principle of Mutual Submission to Marriage Today* by Patricia Gundry, *The Cinderella Complex: Women's Hidden Fear of Independence* by Colette Dowling, *Creative Dislocation* by Robert McAfee Brown, and various other books. After moving to Tennessee, I became active in organizing retreat weekends for Christian singles. We explored what it means to be single and whole. Along the way, I encountered new ideas and had more of my comfortable assumptions questioned, even threatened. But I also began to discover that I could do things. Some of my small challenges became small triumphs. I began to believe that I could survive and not only survive but be happy as a single adult.

Then one evening here at home, Emily came out in her fairy godmother costume, wearing her rhinestone crown and carrying a "magic wand" with a glitter-covered star on the end. She approached me with kindly, fairy-godmother largesse and touched me on the shoulder with her wand, saying, "I am jor (your) fairy godmother. I can make jou anybody jou want to be. Who do jou want to be?"

My first thought was, What an opportunity—to be anybody in the world I want to be—anybody! If only it were true! I decided to play along with the game. But a remarkable thing happened: I couldn't come up with a name to say to my "fairy godmother" because I suddenly realized that I didn't want to be anyone else. I would rather be me than anyone else in the world! I don't think anyone could have been more surprised at that thought than I was. Me, the one who had lived her life as if I were an actor on a stage, continually stepping outside myself to see if I was doing it right, playing my part as I was supposed to, doing what I thought the world wanted, living a script rather than real life—I wanted to be no one else but me? At that moment, I realized that something important had been happening inside me. Divorced, a single parent rearing a child alone, not dating anyone, I still liked myself and couldn't think of anyone I'd rather be than me.

For the first time in my life, I was able to say that being me felt more right than trying to be someone else. For the first time, I realized that I preferred wearing my own armor to trying to clank along in someone else's. And I liked the way that felt!

The armor metaphor goes back to the story of David and Goliath (1 Sam. 17:31-51). You may remember that David killed the giant Goliath with his sling and one smooth stone (v. 17:40). Before that encounter, Saul and some others had tried to prepare David for the battle. David was just a boy, according to the story in First Samuel. He was the youngest of Jesse's many sons, and he couldn't believe that his brothers and even the king were allowing the infidel Goliath to taunt them. David impulsively vowed that he would face the giant and save the day for God's people.

David's brothers thought he was crazy. He was just a boy, after all, not a soldier. Saul, the king, insisted that David wear armor. But, being a shepherd, David had no armor. So he was dressed in Saul's armor, with "a coat of mail" (like knights wear in the King Arthur movies), a helmet, and a sword, the Bible says. He probably also wore greaves, metal plates to protect the legs, since the armor being used in this war included them. (See 1 Samuel 17:6.) Once the soldiers got him all dressed, David couldn't walk. Can you picture it? He's young, probably not "filled out" yet (as we say here in the South), and the armor fitted for Saul, a big man, is so bulky and heavy that David can't move. It must have been a funny sight. David realizes how ridiculous it is for him to try to face the giant in this heavy armor that isn't his, that he isn't used to, and he takes it off. Then he goes out to face Goliath with his sling, with the weapon that is his, that feels right in his hand. It doesn't look like much to the others, but David knows what works for him. David had struggled alone in the wilderness to kill a lion and a bear. He had learned that God would help him and that he could prevail.

In studying that passage, I saw that we often try to wear someone else's armor. That is, we try to face life by being someone we are not. We adopt strategies that work for other people but may not be appropriate for us. We put on a costume and try to be someone other than who we are. Saul's armor was perfectly appropriate for him; it had been made for him. But it was not right for David.

The motives of those who dressed David in the armor were good. They were concerned for his safety, and they wanted to give him the best chance of success that they could. They were trying to help, to protect him and to advance their cause. Wearing chain mail and metal plating was the way they did battle.

The conventions of our society—the manners we learn, the socially approved ways of behaving, the conventions of growing up and marrying—are the way we "do" life. These are tested strategies for facing life, and I had accepted them. But all of them do not fit all of us. This is not to say that the conventions are wrong. They work—most of the time. We know what to expect in certain situations because we know how we "do" this or that. Having these established ways of doing things simplifies life. We know how to behave at weddings, what to wear to church or to work, how to behave in public, because we have learned the rules. Departing from what is familiar in any of these (and a million other situations) can make people uncomfortable.

Change does not come easily, and some of us do not accept it until it is forced upon us. I remember learning in school about the Revolutionary War and why the British troops were so easily routed by the colonists. The British traditionally marched into battle in neat ranks, their weapons at their sides. When they engaged the enemy, they stopped, the front rank knelt, they all raised their weapons, and they fired. The colonists, however, did not march toward the British as was expected of them. Instead, the colonists burst unexpectedly from cover and fired without warning. The formal, British way of doing battle did not work on the frontier. Saul's chain-mail coat did not work for David, and David's sling would not have worked for Saul, I'm sure.

All of the ideas I had absorbed about what I was supposed to be weighed heavily on me for years. I tried to wear other people's armor in myriad ways, from the way I wore my hair to the way I dressed to the way I worshiped. And the weight of all those heavy expectations had often immobilized me and kept me from moving forward. I couldn't walk in someone else's armor. When I tried to live by other people's rules, I could not live my life fully.

David heard a lot from those around him about why he ought to do things differently than he was planning to, but because of what he had learned from his struggles, he understood that their ways wouldn't work for him. Because of his time in the wilderness, he found the courage to try his own way. As I consider David, I believe that I should not try to be someone else. I remind myself of what God has taught me as I struggled alone and trust that God will keep on helping me. My weapons might look flimsy to someone else; my way of approaching life might seem to others to leave me vulnerable. But armor that doesn't fit leaves the wearer vulnerable too. If David had worn a chain-mail coat that folded over because it was too big, arrows could have gotten through and hit him in the torso. A chest or abdominal wound was often fatal. Heavy metal meant to protect him could take away his mobility and leave him at the mercy of an enemy. A sword that was too big for him would be useless, and a helmet that didn't fit could fall over his eyes and obscure his vision. But God gave David a steady arm and an accurate eye to go along with that sling and those five smooth stones. David needed to be able to move freely to use his sling and do what God had sent him to do. Though the veterans around him did not understand this, David trusted his own experience with God.

David's refusal to wear Saul's armor offers a great lesson. The armor we wear has to be our own; our way of approaching life has to be our own. If it is not, we will not be able to use freely the unique gifts and abilities that God has given us. This does not mean we should thumb our noses at suggestions and new possibilities. Armor had to be continually repaired and re-fitted throughout a soldier's life. We also change. Just as the clothes we wore when we were children will not fit us when we are adults, the strategies that work when we are in one place in our lives may not fit when we are in another. We have to continually be open to accepting new armor, to learning new ways of dealing with people and life. (Like me learning to be more conciliatory in the way I express myself—I've come to see that I need to do that.) Having role models and mentors is good. A part of someone else's "armor" might be a great strategy for something we are facing. But always putting aside our personality, our ideas, our needs and desires, is an affront to God. Each of us has a unique part of God to reflect. If we hide that by always presenting ourselves to others in costume, the world will be the poorer for the loss of what we are meant to bring to it. We can trust and value ourselves, including the sling (or the chain mail) that is uniquely ours.

I had come out of my marriage feeling that I was not much of a woman. Being divorced was a huge black mark against me, proof of my inability to do what I was supposed to do. As I heard a character in a movie describe a divorced woman, I was "used goods." I'd be lucky if any other man ever even looked at me. And if no man did, I would be an unhappy and unfulfilled woman, doomed to a bad life. That had been my perspective.

My "fairy godmother" gave me a great gift that night. She helped me to see that I had changed. I had, in fact, come a very long way. I had come to value myself and be happy, without a man in my life and without apology for who I am. Though others may not understand my quirkiness, it is important for me to remember to wear my own armor and not try to force myself into someone else's. God has made me who I am, and though my equipment may look like nothing more than a sling and five smooth stones, it is exactly right for what God wants me to accomplish with my life. My armor fits me just fine, and it is quite comfortable for me. But should I expect less? It was made for me personally by God, who is a great designer.

Like David, we can learn when we're with God in an emotional wilderness, and what we learn is preparation for what is ahead. Both men and women come out of bad marriages feeling as I did. They are unsure of themselves and must work to establish a new identity as a single person. But like me, with time and help from other believers, they do it.

As more and more of us come to the church, it becomes impossible to deny the reality of divorce. We can no longer pretend that everything is all right, that everyone grows up and gets married and lives happily ever after. Those of us who are divorced and in the church are not doing what is expected of us, and most of us are not doing what we expected to be doing. But our presence is also a sign of hope for a good, full life after divorce. We're not following an accepted script; we're writing new stories that are as individual as we are.

---

[1]Kathy Brock, "Some Job Seekers Turn to Surgery to Overcome Bias," *Dallas Business Journal*, vol. 19 no. 7 (October 13, 1995): C7.

[2]Dolly Parton

[3]*The Tennessean* (July 13, 1997): 7B.

[4]"Ballerina's Death Pushes Dancers to Rethink 'Thin'," *The Tennessean* (July 13, 1997): 13A.

[5]Kathy McCoy, *New Teenage Body Book*, Quoted in *USA Today* (July 18, 1997): 8D.

[6]Karen S. Peterson, Quoted in "Knowledgeable Teens Still Starve for Attention," *USA Today* (July 18, 1997): 8D.

[7]Rosemarie Robotham, "What I Learned at Fat Camp," *Walking* (May-June 1997): 70.

CHAPTER 9

THE SHADOW OF
THE VULTURE

If you've driven much on the plains of West Texas in late summer, you've probably seen vultures coasting on the air currents. They circle silently, like remote-controlled black kites, their moving shadows the only variation in color on the flat, brown expanse of ground. Vultures are carrion eaters; they feed on the carcasses of dead animals. When they spot a sick or wounded animal, they coast and they wait. Eventually the animal will collapse, unable to go any further, and die. That's when they move in.

These animals fulfill their role in nature by doing what they do, serving a useful function in the ecosystem. But there is another kind of vulture, another kind of predator, that serves no useful function I have been able to discern. These are the sexual predators.

At the time I divorced, I did not realize that people like these exist almost everywhere. One day when I mentioned a man in the singles group to the singles minister at our church, he said quietly to me, "Be careful of him." I naively asked why.

"Because he's working his way through the women in the group."

"What do you mean by that?"

"I mean, he's one of those men who's carving notches in his belt. Or maybe I should say his headboard."

I thought he was surely mistaken. After all, this was a church group. Why would anyone like that want to be a part of a church group? And the man in question was a vocal, apparently fervent Christian. His name had come up because he'd been circulating in the group a petition to send to our representative in Congress. But why would the minister say something like that without reason? "Why doesn't someone tell him to stay away?" I asked.

"Because we don't tell people to stay away from the church. Besides, all of these people are adults. They make their own choices, and I can't tell them what to do. Just be careful."

I thanked him for the advice but felt sure I would not need it. In all the years of my marriage, I had been approached romantically by only one man, a non-Christian with whom I taught in a public school. No Christian man had ever made improper advances, and I did not expect that to change. I was wrong.

The first time it happened, I was sitting at a table across from a man with whom I worked. He asked me very casually if I were free to enter into sexual liaisons. I thought I had surely misunderstood what he had said, since he was a married man. "I beg your pardon? What did you say?" He repeated his question. I was stunned almost speechless.

Finally I said, "Oh yes, completely free. The catch is, I'm the one who gets to do the choosing—and the ones I choose are few and extremely far between."

His advance took me by surprise. I probably should have told him the answer to that question was none of his business, but I had no prepared response.

Over the years since my divorce, many men have approached me sexually. It happened so many times in the early years that I began keeping a list of their names. I knew otherwise I could not remember how many times it had happened. (It doesn't happen much any more, maybe because I'm older?) Some were work contacts; some I met at conferences or through friends. One particularly persistent man was a co-worker, one of a group with whom I took coffee breaks and went to lunch.

He was married, as were most of the men who approached me, and he tried to convince me that we should have an affair. He used what I know now is a standard line—he and his wife didn't have much of a marriage, he said. They lived in the same house, but they didn't share much else about their lives. They stayed together out of habit and because it was convenient legally and economically and because splitting up would hurt the kids. They had an agreement, he said, that he'd go his way and have his friends, and she would go her way and have her friends.

When he said this, in what I thought was an inspiration, I answered, "Fine. But before we go any further, I'll need to see your signed and notarized copy of the agreement." I was angry at him. I went back to my office still fuming. I went to Tom, my co-worker and good friend, a man of absolute integrity. I had talked with him before about these predatory men and how to deal with them. I said, "It happened again—another married man made a move on me! I am sick of this! I thought he was my friend! Why do they do this?!"

"Stop and think about it," Tom said. "They ARE your friends. It's going to be friends or at least close acquaintances who do this. Total strangers are not going to come up to you and proposition you. These men like you; that's why they want a relationship with you."

But I don't agree with all of that. Men like the ones who hit on me may like me, but they don't want a relationship. They have relationships— long-term commitments—with their wives. What they want from other women is sex that makes no demands on them, that requires no caring and no attention to consequences. There are people who deliberately look for people to take advantage of sexually, and one of the ripe fields for those predators is among people who have recently ended relationships. Singles groups are one of the places such people gather, and so predators come to them.

These encounters are not a matter of overwhelming emotional attraction, of love or even infatuation. They begin with attraction, but it is purely sexual attraction—and we do not have to act on every sexual urge. In order to be faithful to their commitments, to their partners, people of integrity choose not to give in to these impulses. If that were not true, no marriage could withstand the passage of time and the many contacts men and women have with people other than their spouses.

I realized long ago that sexual predators are not looking for love. They are looking for gratification and for disposable people from whom to get it. Of course, the predators do not see things this way. There are those who actually feel they do a service for hurting people by "comforting" them with sexual attention.

A few years ago, a scandal broke when a senator was accused by several women of sexual harassment and exploitation. As more and more women came forward and the charges against him mounted, the senator's diaries were subpoenaed and eventually made public. His own words showed him to be not only a sexual predator but an unwise chronicler of his shenanigans as well. He wrote in graphic detail about sexual encounters with a variety of women. In one entry he wrote about a young woman who confided over dinner that she feared her boyfriend was seeing someone else. The senator wrote in his diary that he was shocked to hear about the boyfriend, since he had had sex with the woman half a dozen times. He commented, "I was feeling sorry for you and thinking I was doing my Christian duty by making love to you. . . . Rather enjoyable . . . but my Christian duty."[1]

It was his "Christian duty"? Does that stun you as it did me? Surely he was being at least partly cynical (as his words show him to have been about many things), but his words help us to understand how these predators rationalize their actions. They theorize that others need sexual attention, and they are more than happy to oblige. They feel that they are doing us poor singles a favor by bedding us. And though married people are approached too, I believe single people are approached more often. After all, with a single person there is no danger of having to confront a jealous spouse.

That some predators consciously choose single people became clear to me several years ago. I was speaking at a Christian conference in another state. Leaders and speakers sat together at meals to assess how the conference was going and to talk about any matters that needed group attention. After the business was done, we visited while we finished the meal. We all enjoyed the time, talking and laughing about the work that brought us together. We talked about our children and our pets and various other things. One night I encountered another of the speakers when I was alone. In what seemed a casual conversation, he asked me what kind of work my husband did, whether he worked in the same field as I. When I said that I was divorced and didn't know what job my former husband currently had, the man became instantly attentive. He told me how long he'd been on the road. He put his arms around me and tried to do more. I managed to stall him and get him to step away from me. Then, as I was trying to figure out how to get rid of him, another speaker walked up. My "admirer" immediately left. The next morning he followed me from the cafeteria and into the building where I was staying. I did not go to my room (because I did not want him to know where it was—obviously some of my naivete was gone) and he finally had to leave to lead a session. I avoided him for the remainder of the conference.

As long as this man thought I was married, he behaved appropriately; but the moment he learned that I was single, he made his move. This was a well-known and married man, a frequent conference presenter. I could not believe what he had done. A few months later, I was talking with a friend at another conference when this man's name came up. I mentioned to her what I had experienced. To my amazement, she said, "Is he still doing that? I can't believe it!"

"Still doing that? STILL? What do you mean?" She went on to tell me that this man was known to approach women at conferences. She told me that someone was supposed to have talked with him about this behavior to get him to stop it. Sadly, I knew that he had not. In fact, this kind of preda-tory behavior is rarely an isolated incident. As we know from various stories that have been in the news, when one person talks publicly about such experiences, others almost always come forward to tell of something similar happening to them with the same person.

I had not previously met the man who made a pass at me during the conference, but I was furious to learn that he was known for this behavior and was continuing to get away with it. After that, I broke the silence about him by privately calling to warn the director of any conference at which I learned he would be speaking. As is often the case, those to whom I spoke either chose not to believe me or not to act on what I told them. I understand their reluctance to accept what I said. We don't want to believe that God's people would behave this way. But if you stop to think about it, the Bible contains many stories of God's people and sexual excess. There are Lot and his daughters, Tamar and her father-in-law, Samson and Delilah, Solomon and his 1000 wives, and others you can probably list. The most famous is probably the story of David and Bathsheba, and it illustrates well many of the issues involved in this problem. The story is told in the book of First Samuel.

There's a war going on, and King David goes to the roof of the palace for a walk. He sees Bathsheba bathing, and he sends for her (2 Sam. 11:2-4). He has sex with her, and when she becomes pregnant, he arranges for her husband Uriah to come home from the front. If Bathsheba has sex with her husband, she can pass the baby off as his, and David's acts will go undis-covered. Uriah is an honorable man, however, and he keeps his soldier's pledge to abstain from sexual contact while at war. David then arranges for Uriah to be put in the front of the fighting and be killed. Once Uriah is dead, David brings Bathsheba to the palace to be one of his harem.

It seems clear that this is not simply an incident of sexual need. David does not need Bathsheba to satisfy his sexual appetites. He has many wives, and if he wanted another new one for variety, he could have chosen from among many willing virgins. But he sees this woman and he wants her. And since he is the king, he can have her. So he sends for her. She is a married woman, which makes his sin even worse, for he commits adultery in the act of exploiting her.

To be completely fair, we must admit possible complicity on Bathsheba's part. With her husband gone, she may have been lonely and felt flattered that the king was interested in her. Having the attention of a powerful man can be exhilarating. But this seems unlikely. She was a woman who kept the religious law even when no one was looking. When David saw her, she was going through the ritual cleansing required by her faith (2 Sam. 11:4). Her husband was an honorable man, and if his family had arranged a good marriage for him, it is likely that Bathsheba was an honorable woman. Realistically, it is unlikely that she could have refused the king's attentions. He was, after all, the king. If she had refused, she could have been killed.

If we put David and Bathsheba's situation in modern terms, David was a man who was using a woman as a diversion. There was a war going on, and maybe this fling was simply a way to forget for a while the affairs of state (forgive the pun). But he wasn't in love; he was in lust. He didn't know the woman; he didn't have a relationship with her, at least not at the beginning of the story. Who she was, was not important—and that may be the saddest part of the whole story. It was not about her; it was about him. Bathsheba suffered great loss because of David's actions. She lost her husband, and then the baby she had conceived with David died. This is not a happy story of two kids who are crazy in love as in one of those romantic comedies we're so fond of. It's a story that shows how destructive sexual predation can be. Bathsheba is taken advantage of, and the consequences are not pretty.

I wish I could say to you that all the people like David live in some other place than you and I do, but the fact is, they don't. Divorced and divorcing people find out the truth of that in many ways. And the predators are not all men. Both men and women are involved. A clergyman friend told me about a day soon after his divorce when five women approached him and offered to comfort him in specific and physical ways. Recently another divorced clergyman told me about a woman in his congregation who called him repeatedly to ask him over "just to talk" while her husband was out of town. In order to make her stop calling, he finally had to be blunt in telling her that what she wanted was not going to happen. And a man in my church who was divorcing (not even officially divorced yet) commented that he was amazed at how many women had already made it clear that they considered him extremely eligible. There are always people like the senator who are willing to do their "Christian duty."

Among singles, we make jokes about "body ministry" regarding people who have this outlook. It is a way of keeping in perspective their absolutely reprehensible behavior. One of the survival skills that we have to learn is saying no in clear and unmistakable ways. That doesn't stop the offers from coming, however, and it doesn't take away the struggle of wanting and needing to feel attractive and lovable—needs and wants of which predators take advantage.

Both men and women talk about feeling like failures when relationships end, and offers of even transitory attention from someone of the opposite sex can sometimes be hard to resist. To those who are frightened that no one will ever find them desirable again, even crumbs of relationship can seem nourishing. When lonely people need someone to hold them and tell them they are okay, they may not stop to think that the kind of people who want to hold them may be thinking of something more than Christian consolation. Predators are not thinking of their prey at all but of themselves.

That's why it is so important to remember David and Bathsheba. Sexually predatory behavior is not about the person being approached. It is about the predator. It is always about the predator. David's attention to Bathsheba was not about her; it was about him. It was about satisfying his desires or alleviating his boredom—either of which is just a way of saying he was using her. Predators use other people as a way of dealing with something that is going on in their lives. David was getting older. He was no longer among those going out to battle "in the spring when kings go out to war" (1 Sam. 11:1, AP). Commanding this woman to come to him and to submit to him was a way to convince himself, at least for a few minutes, that he was still the man he had always been, that he could still make things happen. He used her to make himself feel good. Never mind that he was changing forever the life of an honorable woman. Never mind that she was worried about her husband who had gone off to war. Never mind that there might be disastrous consequences for her. Bathsheba was not important. That is the crux of the using behavior of predators; the object of their attention (and that is what they do—make people into objects) could be anyone. When predators approach, their behavior says the person they approach does not matter. And that is a lie. Each of us does matter. None of us is meant to be disposable. None of us exists merely to provide diversion or anesthesia for another.

But predators become skilled at deceiving vulnerable people. They seek out those who, for whatever reason, may be unable to resist their attention. They look for people so caught up in pain or loss that they forget to take care of themselves. When someone is grieving the loss of a spouse (not just lost through divorce but through death or even a chronic illness), that person's natural defenses may be down. The intuition that often protects us, the sense that tells us something is just not right and we need to be wary, may be suppressed by our pain. Sexual predators know that. They circle like vultures, looking for likely targets. And the reality is that they have done the same thing over and over again. As I write this, the military has gone through a series of scandals and trials about sexual harassment and sexual misbehavior. In most of the cases, after the first victim spoke out, others came forward as well. Sexual predation is a pattern in the lives of those who do it. Anyone will do, anyone at all—which further belittles the importance and worth of their targets. To be approached by someone like this is not a compliment about our beauty or desirability; it is an insult to our intelligence and to our character.

The man who was working his way through the women in our singles group was a type that I find especially disgusting: one of those predators who scout church groups in particular. I'm not sure why they target our groups. Probably part of it is the belief that people in a church group may be safer sexually; those who have fewer sexual partners (and we assume that would be Christians) carry less risk of being infected with sexually transmitted diseases. Part of it may be that they find church people to be more naive, more prone to believe the sad stories they often use to lure their prey into an initial conversation. Whatever the reason, they are part of church groups.

Sexual predators are also part of work groups and social groups and parent groups and school groups. Over the years I have met them in all these places. But Bathsheba's experience helps me to recognize that involvement with them always leads to pain and loss. I've had enough pain and loss already, and that is motivation to avoid them and their advances. Sexually using behavior demeans the user and damages the one being used. When we allow a user to continue in that behavior, we allow her or him to continue to avoid the real issues that underlie it. We delay their healing and growth, and we allow ourselves to be hurt. I am a worthwhile person, dearly loved by God, and God wants me to take care of myself. God wants me to love myself and protect myself from all those who would use me.

God wants that for each of us.

---

[1]John Aloysius Farrell, "Senator's Diaries Offer Peek into Seamy, Cynical World," Quoted in the *Denver Post* (September 8, 1995): 24A.

CHAPTER 10

"YOU'RE NOBODY 'TILL SOMEBODY LOVES YOU"

Jesus, tired from his journey, is resting by a well in the village of Sychar, in Samaria. John 4:4 tells us that Jesus "had to" go through Sameria, perhaps in order to have the encounter that we read about in the next verses. As Jesus waits for the disciples, a woman comes to the well to draw water. It is the middle of the day, not usually the time that women come to the village wells, but this woman approaches. As she does, Jesus asks her to give him a drink. The woman, surprised, says, "How is it that you, a Jew, ask a drink of me?"

Jesus would have had at least two reasons to remain silent. First, in that culture, men did not speak to women in public. Rabbis especially did not speak to women, and Jesus was a rabbi. Second, the woman was a Samaritan. As she reminds Jesus, Jews do not have anything to do with Samaritans. But Jesus says to her, "If you knew the gift of God, . . . you would have asked [me]"(v. 10).

That is an outrageous statement in this context. A woman would not have approached a man. Even more, a Samaritan woman would not have approached a Jewish man with a request. What could possibly be important enough to cause her to break the social rules? But Jesus goes on to tell the woman, "Anyone who drinks the water from this well will thirst again, but those who drink of the water I give will never thirst again" (vv. 13-14, AP).

The woman, being practical, says, "Sir, give me this water, so I will never be thirsty and won't have to keep coming here every day to get water" (v. 15, AP) At this point, Jesus goes back to traditional ways and asks the woman to go and get her husband before the conversation continues. He wants to talk about spiritual things, and so he must speak to the man, not to the woman. But she hedges, not quite lying but not quite telling the truth either, saying, "I have no husband."

Jesus responds, "You are right in saying, 'I have no husband'; for you have had five husbands, and the one you have now is not your husband" (v. 17-18).

Confronted with this information about her personal life, the woman retreats from that subject and begins talking theology. If it's a choice between talking about her personal life, which is taboo, and talking about religion, another taboo for a woman, she chooses to talk about religion. And that's fine with Jesus, for he really wants to talk with her about what it means to worship God. The talk about the other things has opened this door.

This story is familiar to many of us. The Samaritan woman becomes a symbol for Jesus' desire to reach out to all people, not just the Jews. But like the personal information about the prophets that is woven into their prophecies, woven into this theological discussion is a story of a woman who has been in and out of many relationships.

Sermons about this story usually include the theory that the woman came to the well in the middle of the day in order to avoid the respectable women of the village. She may have been an outcast, someone looked down on by her neighbors. At the least she was sensitive enough about her living arrangement that she did not want to talk with Jesus about it.

This woman brings a message about a deep hunger for relationship. She has been married five times. Do you know anyone who has been married and divorced several times? I do. We make assumptions (and comments) about people like that, but in Jesus' time the situation was more extreme. Women were dependent on their fathers and then their husbands for sustenance and protection. An unmarried woman was a vulnerable woman. Women could be divorced for any reason; if a woman displeased her husband in any way, she could be put aside. If a woman was barren, her husband could divorce her. The Bible doesn't say why this woman had been put aside by five husbands (only men could divorce; women could not initiate it), but surely she has been deeply hurt. Imagine being rejected by five husbands in succession. Her self-esteem was probably in tatters. This was a small town too, and people in small towns know nearly everything about everybody. And what they don't know, they suppose about, speculating in ways that fit in with their ideas of what is probable.

It could not have been easy for her to bear the stigma of having been put aside as many times as she had. Public opinion notwithstanding, however, when Jesus met her she was living with yet another man, one to whom she was not married. This man may not have wanted to marry her. But it is also possible that she was the one who didn't want to get married. Perhaps she had finally given up on the ideal of lasting love, despairing of ever finding anyone who could love her as she was and remain committed to her. Whatever her reasons and her emotional state, she shows us that people keep reaching out, keep looking for love, even when they've been hurt by relationships over and over again.

And a lot of us are like that woman. "You're Nobody 'Till Somebody Loves You" is more than a song title; in many ways, it's one of our cultural beliefs. Finding someone to love us is validation. Being in a relationship is proof that we are worthwhile and okay. A co-worker once said to me, "A bad husband is better than no husband at all," as if nothing could be worse than being alone. The saddest part of that exchange is that she's not the only one who feels that way.

It seems obvious that we value relationships. The plethora of books on the subject is proof of that. People want relationships and are looking for ways to make them better. There are books about relationship addiction, books about how to find and marry a rich man (I don't know that there's one about how to marry a rich woman, but there probably is), a zillion books about how to communicate with those we love (and those we don't). We are definitely interested in relationships.

But sometimes we approach romantic relationships as if they are the key to our lasting happiness. There's an old rock-and-roll song in which the singer claims that once the lucky couple goes to the chapel and gets married they will "never be lonely anymore." Though we can't turn to popular music for our theology, this attitude is pervasive in our culture. Actress Rene Russo (*Ransom, Lethal Weapon 3, Tin Cup, Get Shorty, In the Line of Fire*) said in an interview, "People think, 'If I just had a mate, my life would be so wonderful.'"[1] The hit movie *Waiting to Exhale* (based on Terry McMillan's best-selling novel by the same name) follows four women who are searching for good relationships (mostly unsuccessfully). Savannah, one of the four, is pressured by her mother to renew a relationship with a par- ticular man—who happens to be married. ("Even a married man is better than no man at all?" to paraphrase my co-worker.) When Savannah asks, "Mama, why are you doing this?" her mother tells her that she just doesn't want her daughter to be alone.

Sometimes I think the church has adopted the same attitude. The headline in a denominational newspaper reads, "Apart, we're less than one; together, we're more than two" over an article about strengthening mar- riages. Of course strengthening marriages is a worthwhile goal, but this headline says we are less than whole if we are alone, that who we are depends on other people.

I felt that way after my divorce. I struggled with feeling that my identity had disappeared. I didn't know how to be Mary Lou the single person. When I was by myself, I didn't know who I was. I had never spent much time alone. As one of seven kids, I grew up in a household where there were always people around—my siblings and their friends, cousins and neighborhood children. When I went off to college, I lived in a dormitory and had a roommate. Then I married. Even after the divorce, I had Emmy to care for about half the time. I did not know how to be comfortable being alone. Even more important, I didn't want to be alone. When I was alone, I found myself reflecting on my life, my situation, and I didn't want to do that. Once I began coming out of the depression that followed the divorce decree, I felt that too much introspection might be dangerous. I didn't want to wallow in self-pity.

So I did the only thing I could think of: I began filling my time with activities. They were all worthwhile, of course. The church always needs volunteers and can keep them busy. I threw myself into involvement with the class for single adults. I told myself it was important to stay busy in order to keep my mind off myself. Even when I was weary at the end of a long week of work and graduate school and caring for Emily, I made myself attend the activities. I began a Bible study with some other single women. I pitched in when our class "adopted" a needy family and spent time in their home, getting to know them and building a friendship with them. I was very busy running from myself. Deep down, I was afraid to look long and hard at who I was. What if I did and decided I could not stand what I saw?

But God the opportunist, as always taking advantage of the tiniest opening that we allow, came to guide me. God used one of my close friends in the singles group to coax me into a process of discovery. Karen began memorizing the Sermon on the Mount. (That's three chapters—chapters, not verses—in the Gospel of Matthew.) When our core group of five or six was together, she'd hand one of us her Bible and say, "Check me on this." Then she'd begin reciting. I asked her why she was memorizing this long passage, and she told me about a Bible study she'd attended. The leader had told a story about some Christian people in another country, I think political prisoners, who had only one Bible among them. They decided to each one memorize a significant portion of scripture so that when their one remaining Bible was taken away they could still hear God's word. The leader had challenged the people in the Bible study group, saying, "If your Bible were taken from you, would you know enough of it to be able to comfort yourself and others?" Karen decided that she would not, so she chose to begin memorizing.

Because of her example, I decided to begin memorizing Paul's Letter to the Colossians. Here's where God's opportunism becomes clear: I did it partly because I did not want Karen to outdo me. After all, her recitations were pretty impressive. God used my pride to reach me—and ultimately to change me.

The Letter to the Colossians contains several of my favorite Bible verses. That's why I chose it. One of the repeated ideas in this letter is what it means to be "in Christ" and to have Christ live in us. I began my memorizing with chapter 3 because the first two verses talk about applying both our hearts and our minds to our life in Christ. That speaks especially to me because I believe faith is a matter of both affections (our heart) and will (setting our minds). I tried to memorize one phrase at a time. Each night before going to sleep, I began by reviewing what I had memorized up to that point. Sometimes I wrote out the passage; sometimes I repeated it aloud. After reviewing, I repeated the additional phrase over and over until I thought I had it memorized. Then I repeated again all that I had memorized, adding the new phrase.

It took me quite a while to memorize each verse. It took months, in fact, to finish that one chapter. I thought I was simply memorizing; I did not realize the power this discipline has and the power of God's word to form us. While I was repeating the words, the message was sinking into my heart. It goes back to the first verses of chapter three—as I used my mind, my heart was also affected. When I came to verse 11, I felt as if my eyes were being opened. That verse says that in our Creator "there is no longer Greek and Jew, circumcised and uncircumcised, barbarian, Scythian, slave and free; but Christ is all and in all!" This verse showed me that cultural differences don't matter, what religious laws we keep and what rituals we observe (or don't) don't matter, social status or occupation don't matter. Even marital status and our cultural attitudes about it don't matter. In fact, where this same list appears in Paul's Letter to the Galatians, "male and female" is added. Not even that matters to God. As Colossians 3:3 says, our lives are "hidden with Christ in God." Day after day, week after week, as I repeated Colossians 3:11, my attitude about myself was changing. I began to entertain the idea that my being "in Christ" was the most important determinant of who I am as a person. It was even more important than the fact that I was divorced.

I continued to meditate (that's what the continual repeating of the words amounted to) on the Letter to the Colossians. Colossians says that Christ is in all of creation, that "without him was not anything made that was made" and that in him "all things hold together." Christ is the glue of the universe, the one who holds things in their proper relationship to one another. Without him nothing would last. But the most important phrase for me comes from Colossians 2:10, which says that we "are complete in him" (KJV). Christ is my completion. I am not complete in being married or being a mother or being a writer or anything else. Only in Christ am I complete, and Christ is all I need to be complete. Whether or not I ever had another relationship with a man, I was already complete because I was "in Christ."

This is a hard idea to square with much of what we see and hear. Some people feel good about themselves and fully alive only when they are in a romantic relationship. Some feel alive only during the infatuation phase of relationships, that initial euphoria when they are madly in love, before reality sets in. I read something that likened the excited feelings of infatuation to the adrenalin rush that allows a tiny woman to lift a car when someone she loves is trapped under one. Infatuation can also be like the rush of endorphins that helps athletes push themselves to incredible lengths. There's no doubt that being in love feels wonderful and that loving and being loved by another person enriches life. But those relationships do not define who we are.

Think again about the woman at the well. Like me, she was apparently not eager to look closely at who she was. When Jesus asked her about her husband, she changed the subject. She did not want to talk about relationships. But Jesus wanted to talk about precisely that. He wanted to direct her to the one relationship that could give her what she needed and what we all need. The only relationship that lasts, that will never disappoint us, that will change us and energize us from the inside out, is the relationship that God offers. Only God can give us genuine life that feels like a spring of fresh water gushing up from deep inside us. Unlike infatuation and euphoria, the life God gives us, lasts. Jesus talks to this woman person-to-person, not about her failures but about a relationship that will satisfy her deepest longings.

He tells her that God seeks those who will worship "in spirit and in truth." At least a part of worshiping God "in truth" is coming to God as we are. We don't have to hide from knowing ourselves and from letting God know us. Just as Jesus spoke to this woman about her life and her longings honestly and without condemnation, he welcomes me. With the woman at the well, a remarkable thing happens. She leaves her water jar and seeks out the people of Sychar. Leaving the water jar reveals a shift in her priorities—she is no longer preoccupied with daily needs—but approaching the people of the city reveals a change in her perception of herself as well. She is no longer hiding from the townspeople; on the contrary, she seeks them out. She has found someone who welcomes her just as she is and who believes she can enter into relationship with God as fully as anyone else. The facts about marital status are trivial alongside the truth that God is seeking us and wants relationship with us.

I came to see that as long as I seek in human relationships what I can get only from God, my identity is up for grabs. Being Emily's mother, Spencer's wife, a writer, or anything else I might say defines who I am could be gone in an instant. If I depend on these roles or relationships for my identity, without them I am nobody. The only identity that life cannot take from us is our identity in God. It is a privilege to have people to love and a privilege to be part of their lives, to value them and support them. But we cannot depend on others for our happiness or our identity.

People are only human, and so ultimately they will always disappoint us. Whether the failure is a failure of energy or caring or insight or constancy, there will come a time when humans will fail us. They won't be able to be there when we need them or understand when we need them to understand or keep their commitments to us in some other way. There will also come times when we fail others—as I did in my marriage and as I have many times as a parent. But I am complete in Christ. The only place I am complete is in Christ, and the only stable identity is my identity in him. As I learn more about myself in relation to Christ, I am able to build healthier and stronger relationships with others. The answers to all our questions about relationships are found in owning before God who we are—worshiping "in truth"—and welcoming others to do the same (John 4:24). Their identity does not come from us, and ours does not come from them.

Looking back, I can see that a clearer sense of my identity and worth in my youth and young adulthood might have kept me from getting into the kinds of relationships that I did. If I had taken time to know myself, I might have known better what I needed and wanted in relationships with others. I could also have better protected myself from pressures to try to be someone other than who I am. There's an old story about a sculptor who's asked how to sculpt an elephant. He answers, "Oh, it's easy. You just get a big block of stone and chip away everything that doesn't look like an elephant." Part of maturing as a person is determining for ourselves what looks like the work of art we are meant to be and what doesn't.

It's sort of like having a personal mission statement. There is value in having clear priorities and goals. We've heard about businesses with mission statements, hospitals with mission statements posted in their lobby, church mission statements, and so on. We have a mission statement for the singles program in my church. At least one personal management system advocates writing a family mission statement and having each one in the family write a personal mission statement. Then when someone is asked to do something, that person can consult her or his mission statement and the family mission statement as a guide. If the request fits in with what the family and the person have identified as their mission (and the family/person has time for what is asked), the person being asked may agree. But if the task or activity doesn't fit, the person can say no without guilt. This level of focus and self-awareness helps in making decisions and in choosing friends and companions. Suppose someone were to approach you and ask you to enter a dating relationship. If your personal mission statement named working on relationships with family as first priority for the next year, you could be honest in saying that. You might propose a limited friendship with this new person, outlining in advance how much time and what level of commitment you are willing to give. Though the mission-statement approach may sound a bit cold-hearted, we all make choices like this all the time. We just do it without a formal framework.

We have to make choices because there is always going to be more to do than we can ever do. There are more people to care for than we could ever reach. Good causes abound. Nice people abound. But we cannot do all that needs to be done or be in relationship with every nice person on the planet. We are finite. Though God calls everybody to do something, God doesn't call anybody to do everything. We will never be able to respond to all the invitations that come at us, but the good news is that we are not meant to.

A sense of what God wants us to do and to be allows us to more easily push away the things that aren't right for us. If I have a sense of who I am, I can identify what "doesn't look like an elephant." When I hold in my heart a clear sense of myself as infinitely valued by and valuable to God, I can resist when someone crosses my boundaries or mistreats me or intrudes on who I am. I can choose more wisely in relationships. I can treat myself like I am somebody—because I am! And so are we all, for each one of us is and always has been a dearly loved child of God. This is our true identity, one that cannot be taken from us. Each one of us is truly somebody.

We long for happiness. We long to feel loved and valued, and it is comforting to think that if we can just find the right person, all will be well. I suppose it would be possible to move from relationship to relationship for an entire lifetime, looking for that perfect person. But at its root that hunger is a spiritual hunger that can never be satisfied by another person. The hunger to be completely known and completely loved can be satisfied ultimately only by allowing ourselves to be known by God. As Augustine of Hippo said to God long ago, "Thou hast made us for thyself, and our heart is restless until it rests in thee." The woman at the well was searching for something she could not even identify; she only knew that it had something to do with God. Jesus' response to her shows us that that is enough. God responds to our hunger for relationship because it is God who places that hunger within us and uses it to woo us into relationship with Christ. There we find our wholeness. And wholeness is the key to good relationships.

You may have heard married people refer to one another as "my better half." Hearing that always bothers me because when it comes to relationships, two halves do not make a whole. Only two whole people can make a whole relationship. Finding our identity and wholeness in Christ frees us to build healthy, wholesome relationships in a way that nothing else can. Our identity in Christ is the only identity that is completely secure, the identity that can never be taken from us, and it is the source of our wholeness.

----

[1]Rene Russo in Jeffrey Zaslow's column "Straight Talk," *USA Weekend* (May 16-18, 1997): 22.

CHAPTER 11

STEPPIN' OUT
AND MOVIN' ON

Having said all that I did in the last chapter about finding our identity and wholeness in Christ alone, I want also to acknowledge that we need relationships with other people. As much as we need God, because we are human we also need other people. Adventurer Steven Callahan wrote strikingly about this in his book *Adrift: Seventy-Six Days Lost at Sea*. After his sailboat went down west of the Canary Islands, Callahan found himself drifting in an inflatable raft with very little food or water. He endured incredible experiences as he waited for some ship to see him. After surviving a storm, he wrote of the peace he found in his simple existence:

> As I look out of the raft, I see God's face in the smooth waves, His grace in the dorado's swim, feel his breath against my cheek as it sweeps down from the sky. I see that all of creation is made in His image. Yet despite His constant company, I need more. I need more than food and drink. I need to feel the company of other human spirits. I need to find more than a moment of tranquility, faith, and love. A ship, Yes, I still need a ship.[1]

He became aware of his need for other people in an unforgettable way. For most of us the process is less dramatic, but the need is the same. Some of us are more aware of this need than others are. Some of us need only one or two close friendships to feel that our lives are full. Some of us need to be with people during the process of healing from loss, and some of us need solitude before we are ready to go out in public again.

When we decide to try to build new relationships, we approach them with widely varying assumptions and expectations. I divorced believing that I would not ever marry again. But I never understood that to mean that there would be no relationships with men in my life. I like men. I like them a lot. All my life I have had male friends. Growing up with four brothers, I spent lots of time with males and learned to enjoy their company. I knew that I wanted and needed male companionship—eventually.

But I told myself that I would take a year off before I began dating. Though no one told me so, I knew somehow that I needed time without romantic relationships in my life. I needed time to sort out my feelings and to regain my emotional equilibrium.

Questions of when to date and whom to date are popular topics in all the groups of Christian singles that I've been part of. Another favorite topic of discussion is what the Bible tells us about how to conduct ourselves as single men and women. We all wish it told us more. But the Bible is silent on many subjects. It does not specifically address space travel, organ donation, birth control, or AIDS. It is silent on these and many other issues because it was written in another time and in other cultures. It is important to remember that as we read. For instance, Hebrew scripture shows us a culture that assumes marriage and gives men power over women, grouping women with property (see Exodus 20:17). Non-marriage, widowhood, and barrenness are all pictured as strongly negative. We should not expect to read much about relationships among single people because the culture that gave us the Bible didn't expect people to choose singleness or to remain single.

The New Testament says more about singleness, but not about singleness as we experience it in the late 1990s. The Apostle Paul, who wrote most of what we quote from the epistles when we talk about relationships, believed that Christ would return within his lifetime, and so he advised everyone to remain as they were. Those who were married were to remain married; those who were single were to remain single; those who were slaves were to remain slaves and not seek their freedom. It wasn't going to be long until Christ returned, Paul thought, and therefore social situation did not matter. Essentially Paul told his readers not to waste their energy on these peripheral matters but to use every minute to spread the gospel, to draw in as many as possible before Christ returned—which would be very, very soon. If he had known that it was going to be two thousand years, he might had given different advice. But he didn't know that we were going to be living together as Christian men and women for at least a couple of millennia. He didn't know that a third of the United States population over eighteen was going to be single. But it is, and though the Bible does not address our situation directly, single believers can find help in the principles underlying its stories.

A primary story about relationships is that of Adam and Eve. In both creation stories, the one in Genesis 1:26–2:3 and the one in Genesis 2:4-25, male and female are linked together from the moment of their creation. In the Genesis 1 story, they are linked together by function. They are told to continue the race by reproducing and to care for the earth and the animals. The story in Genesis 2 links male and female by emotional needs. In this story God sees the man and says, "It is not good that the man should be alone; I will make him a helper as his partner" (Gen. 2:18). We see here a God who cares for the creation and who recognizes our need not just for physical sustenance but for companionship.

In fact, this need is built into us. God wants relationship with us; and so, being made in God's image, we too desire relationships. Many of us echo God's statement that it is not good to be alone; it doesn't feel right. We don't like it. And there is nothing wrong with that. It is not a defect that we yearn for relationship; we were created to be this way.

This universal need is fodder for much of the entertainment industry, and to look at all the magazine articles and books on relationship, for much of the publishing industry as well. Seinfeld, a situation comedy about single adults, was among the recent number-one television shows.[2] One episode of Seinfeld that I saw included a conversation between Jerry and George about an idea for a television show. They discussed a show that sounded remarkably like Seinfeld, concluding that it was a show "about nothing." Seinfeld is not number one because it's a show about nothing. It's number one because it's a show about community and about the difficult search for lasting relationships. It is what entertainment calls an "ensemble" show, where a continuing small cast carries the story line. Episode after episode, viewers tune in to see Jerry or George or Elaine or Kramer search for or begin or end a romance. And when they fail (as they always do), they comfort one another.

In 1996, Seinfeld and E.R. became the first regular network series in history to sell a thirty-second commercial for a million dollars.[3] Advertisers are willing to pay that much because of the size of the audience. Having so many people tune in is evidence that a large part of our population identifies with the content of the show. Many of us share their frustrations, and we welcome the chance to be able to laugh at the situations.

Or think about the movies that are box-office smashes. Aside from the disaster/extreme-hero movies (and most of these have a sub-plot of some kind of romance), the ones studios bet on are the romantic comedies.

Critics quoted in newspaper ads on the movie page always seem to dub some movie the "romantic comedy of the summer" or "of the season." Moviemakers keep producing these films because they know people will pay to see them. And people pay to see them because they're wrestling with the same struggles as the characters and they want to be able to laugh about them. As Mother used to say, "Sometimes you have to laugh to keep from crying."

The Bible gives us many stories that show the same struggles. We see in its pages that relationships between men and women can be sexually driven and violent (Samson and Delilah, Tamar and Amnon); they can be manipulative and exploitive (Rebekah and Isaac, David and Bathsheba); they can be instructive and strengthening (Deborah and Barak, Esther and Mordecai; Huldah and Josiah); they can be supportive and redemptive (Joseph and Mary, Ruth and Boaz, Mary Magdalene and Jesus). They can be tangled (Abraham, Hagar, and Sarah; Leah, Rachel, and Jacob); they can show the power of love (Jacob and Rachel). The Bible shows too that deception, trickery, and disaster are sometimes part of relationships. But one truth that I see in all the stories is this: God uses human relationships. God uses our interactions with others to shape us, and our relationships are woven into what God is doing in the world. We may be unaware of it, but as we muddle along, God is at work through the daily exchanges we have with others. Ultimately, that is why relationships deserve our attention.

Though we are designed for relationships, finding good ones can be difficult because of the obstacles we encounter in our search. One of these obstacles is unfinished business from the past. We may more easily recognize it as fear and mistrust or as bitterness and anger. Sometimes hurts we have suffered in the past make us wary of trusting others. We may fear that we will fail again or that we will be rejected. Clues that this may be the case are avoiding relationships completely or holding back from being ourselves in new relationships.

Sometimes we have unresolved anger, of which we may or may not be consciously aware. The anger and frustration that comes from troubled relationships may go underground, emerging in things like jokes about dumb blondes, the "old ball and chain," and testosterone poisoning. This underground anger also appears in situation comedies that show smart women making dupes of men (the *I Love Lucy* approach) or smart men making dupes of women (the old Rock Hudson–Doris Day movies like *Pillow Talk* and its clones).

Anger also comes out in blanket statements such as, "All men are jerks!" or "Women only care about getting you to the altar. After that it's all downhill." Sentences that start "All men . . ." or "All women . . ." may be a clue to unresolved anger. When a former partner can still push our buttons and get us upset (as I have mentioned was true for me), that's a sign of unresolved feelings. These can sabotage current relationships because in weak moments we may dump old feelings on new partners. The only way to prevent that from happening is to deal with the feelings. We may do this through prayer and journaling, or we may seek out a counselor for more formal help. Whatever approach works, the time and effort are worth it because of the freedom that comes when we stop the past from controlling us in the present.

A second obstacle to healthy relationships is destructive patterns. They may be destructive patterns within us, such as choosing inappropriate partners, refusing to acknowledge problems, choosing abusive partners, refusing to communicate, and refusing to deal with conflict. They may also be destructive patterns in others, patterns such as addiction to work or alcohol and drugs or spending. If we realize we are thinking, "Oh no! Not again!" or "Wait a minute. Something about this feels awfully familiar," we may be caught in an old pattern. Another clue is having friends point out in conversation that they have had this same conversation with us before; only the names are different. I have a friend whom I'll call Sean who called to talk some months ago. I asked about his relationship with his significant other, whom I have met only once. He said there were problems. She was seeing another man at the same time she was seeing him, as his wife had done during their marriage, and he was feeling betrayed and rejected. As he talked, it came out that this new significant other worked in the same profession as his former wife. Then it came out that she had done something else his wife had done, and something else. I stopped him and said, "Let me just recap, OK?" One by one I listed about five similarities between this relationship and the former one. "Does any of this sound vaguely familiar to you, my friend?" He admitted that it did. In all their manifestations, destructive patterns interfere with fullness of life.

A third category of obstacles is unrealistic expectations. There are no perfect people out there, and if there were we would avoid them, since none of us is perfect. I used to play a psychological game in my relationships with men, that I call "Blemish." In this game, after dating for a while, I would begin looking for faults so I could begin stepping back from commitment. I would keep looking until I found some "fatal flaw." That kept me safe from having to think about a long-term relationship. If every person we meet is somehow not quite right, we may be dealing with unrealistic expectations. Another clue is daydreaming about Prince Charming or Sleeping Beauty or some mythical, perfect person who's out there waiting for us to discover him or her. Feeling disappointed about small disagreements or falling into all-or-nothing thinking ("If we can't agree on this, the relationship is doomed!") may be clues that we are looking for relationships that are always smooth and free of conflict—which is unrealistic and which can end good relationships. All relationships hit snags, and all relationships take work. Anyone who says otherwise will probably lie about other things. Searching for a relationship that offers uninterrupted bliss is unrealistic. As a friend said to me years ago, "In every relationship, someone has to change the baby's diapers and take out the garbage." In other words, good relationships have to fit in with real life. They have to deal with practical considerations and that means the unpleasant as well as the pleasant parts of life. If we don't want to admit that, we are being unrealistic.

Another obstacle to good relationships is unmet basic needs. The psychologist Abraham Maslow gave us what is known as the "hierarchy of needs," a concept that places categories of needs in a progression. At the base of the hierarchy are the biological needs for food and water, for survival. The next level is the need for safety and security. The third level is the need for love and belongingness—for social affiliation. The fourth level is esteem needs, self-esteem and esteem from others (social status). The highest level of need in Maslow's scheme is the need for self-actualization.[4] This is the level where the individual reaches her or his highest individual potential and is able to be altruistic, to reach out to others without self-interest and do good without needing to be recognized for it.

Maslow's theory is important for me because he derived his theory from the study of healthy people (rather than from the study of those with adjustment problems, such as those studied by Freud). Among healthy people, all these needs exist. Maslow said that higher-level needs cannot be met until lower-level needs are satisfied. This means that we cannot turn our attention to our needs for love and belongingness until our survival and safety needs are met. If we feel unsafe physically or emotionally, we cannot fully relate socially. For instance, in an abusive setting where people do not feel physically safe, they cannot freely love themselves or love others. If our self-esteem needs are not met, we cannot reach out to love others selflessly;

we may use others to get affirmation for ourselves rather than valuing them for their own uniqueness.

When we cannot trust others, when we do not feel safe, when we fear rejection, when we are so concerned about getting our own needs met that we cannot consider the needs of others, we are blocked in building healthy relationships. Chronic anxiety about life in general is often evidence of unmet basic needs. When I was struggling with low self-esteem during and after my marriage, counseling was an avenue of God's healing grace for me. I believe almost everyone can benefit from counseling after loss, especially children. I've read lots of articles and books that say children often blame themselves for their parents' divorce and feel scared and insecure. Talking with an understanding, uninvolved adult can help them to make sense of their feelings and to feel good about themselves. If they and we do not confront our needs and find ways to meet them, we can't move toward our best in relationships.

The fifth category of obstacle is one that I call simply "life." Relationships require time and energy (and usually money), and we have to be realistic about our limits. We need balance between work and play, solitude and sociability, giving care and receiving it. (See Ecclesiastes 3:1-8 for the Bible's view on this.) Sometimes meeting needs for relationship must take second place to other responsibilities and needs for a while. ("For a while" is a key phrase; ignoring our own needs long-term is not good for us and therefore not good for our relationships.) Someone who is in school and holding down a job or working and caring for young children or struggling with financial problems and keeping a home functioning may find there is no energy left over for relationships. During Emily's pre-school years, a nice man was interested in me. I was working hard at a new job and juggling the demands of single parenting. Every time he came over, I fell asleep. I fell asleep sitting on the sofa, so I moved to the floor beside the fireplace and fell asleep there. I fell asleep talking to him on the phone. I finally had to acknowledge to myself that I just couldn't manage a relationship at that time in my life. When the stress of getting ready for a date outweighs the pleasure of going out, life may be telling us to rest from relationships for a while. If we can't remember what day it is, we don't have clean clothes to wear (and where is it I'm supposed to be going, anyway?), and we forget to pick up the children (I did that once too), we may be in a time when life stands in the way of relationships. Putting aside relationship needs temporarily may sometimes be the sensible and mature course of action.

There are also two dangers connected to the question of relationships. The first is that we may turn off our emotions and push others away. The actor Pierce Brosnan, whose wife Cassie died of ovarian cancer several years ago, put it well. When an interviewer asked him about the possibility of loving again, Mr. Brosnan said it can happen, "If you don't let your heart close down," but then he added, "It's very difficult to do."[5] Great pain can tempt us to hold back from caring in order to avoid hurting again. But the saying "Sorrow stretches out a place in the heart for joy" implies that great sorrow can enlarge our capacity to feel joy. If we can allow ourselves to trust God's goodness, we can find the courage to risk caring again. Grace floods into our lives in the love we receive from others, and shutting ourselves off from others can shut us off from joy that God wants to bring us.

The second danger is jumping too soon into serious relationships. A scene in the movie *When Harry Met Sally* shows Sally (Meg Ryan) upset when she learns that her former long-time boyfriend is marrying "Kimberley," his young, new love. Crying loudly and wiping her nose, Sally says, "This isn't supposed to happen! She's supposed to be his transitional person. He isn't supposed to marry her!" The "transitional person" is a familiar character in singles circles. A transitional person is the first person with whom one has a relationship after a former relationship has ended. A transitional person helps us through the adjustment period when we are learning to see ourselves as a single rather than as half of a couple. Some people seem to specialize in relationships with those freshly out of other relationships.

Some people, however, are very clear that that role is not for them. My friend Valerie was at a party soon after she had filed for divorce. She met an attractive man, and they chatted. He finally asked her if she was single and if he could call her sometime about going out. She said that she was in the process of divorcing. He reached into his pocket, handed her a business card, and said, "Call me when your decree is eighteen months old." He believed, rightly, that people need time to settle old issues before taking on the new ones that come with new relationships.

A transitional person is not a bad idea. Someone trying to forge a new identity may need a friend who will listen for hours to re-telling of the stories about the crumbling (or bombing) of a relationship. For many people, baring their soul to someone who will listen makes them feel that they have rediscovered or found for the first time the intimacy they need. The listener may feel the same way. (The apparent listener/confidante may also be a predator who adopts this pose as a technique for getting the prey's defenses down. That cynical view reflects reality.) But very often, one or the other of the people in such a relationship may not know that the other sees him or her as a transitional person, someone to help with the adjustment to single life. If one person or the other starts to push for a more serious relationship, someone may be wounded by rejection. Even worse, one person may pressure the other into marrying. Very often, within weeks or at most months of such a marriage both persons know they have made a mistake, and they separate. This happens so often that there is a name for it; it's called a "whoops." A "whoops" is a very short second (or third) marriage that comes right after the end of one relationship and just before the end of another one.

It is easy to understand why people fall into these situations. The months or years when a marriage is disintegrating are often very lonely for both partners. Once the marriage ends, newly single people may find it difficult to figure out the difference between genuine compatibility and simple relief from loneliness. In these situations, Matthew's advice in another context to be "wise as serpents and harmless as doves" (v. 10:16, KJV) is good counsel. We must be wise in assessing our own needs and what we need in relationships. We don't do this cold-heartedly, as if we were grading meat. We do it because as Christians we want to do no harm to others; on the contrary, we want to do good. In relationships, that means finding persons for whom we can be good partners and who will call forth the best in us. As with Adam and Eve, we need to find a partner who is the right fit, one whose characteristics and personality fit with our own. It may take a while to figure out what that means, especially if we were married for many years and have not taken stock of all the changes that have happened in us. Someone who might have been right when we were twenty may not be right when we are forty or sixty.

People often want to know how long they should wait after the end of a relationship before beginning to date. That's like asking how long it takes to read a book. What's the book, and who's doing the reading? Leo Tolstoy's *War and Peace* at over 1,000 pages will take considerably longer to read than a romance novel—no matter who's doing the reading, but the size of the task and the approach of the person doing it make a difference. A good reader with some background in history will make it through *War and Peace* considerably faster than a beginning reader. In a similar way, getting over a relationship depends on what the person involved brings to it. The end of a long-term relationship is a loss that needs to be mourned, but it's not the same as a marriage. A two-year marriage where the couple has no children leaves the former spouses with less baggage than a thirty-year marriage of a couple who have children and grandchildren. The death of a spouse leaves the remaining partner in a different situation than a divorce.

And people deal differently with loss, just as people read differently. Someone who reads *War and Peace* steadily and consistently for thirty minutes every night will get to the end faster than someone who reads a few pages every few months. Someone who works diligently at recovering from the loss of a love may make faster progress than someone who avoids thinking about or dealing with the pain and the relationship issues. But it is not merely a matter of effort, either. Emotional work is draining and doesn't necessarily proceed in a direct line. Some people may need counseling after the end of a relationship, and some may work intensively for a while and then need to take a break from the intensity. The work of healing varies. It may be a long while before some people are ready. (In all the years I've been involved in singles ministry, I have never seen a person remarry within two years of the end of a previous marriage and have the second marriage last.) But deciding when the time is right is a personal decision, one to be made after prayer and careful consideration.

After my marriage ended, I determined that before I dated anyone I needed to decide what was important to me, what I saw as the essentials. I did not want to repeat the mistakes I had made in earlier relationships; I believe the maxim that those who do not learn from history are doomed to repeat it.

So I decided that in the cool light of solitude, before I was involved with anyone (and subject to being swayed by my emotions), I would make a list of the traits I wanted and needed in a partner. That may sound calculating, but I believe God wants us to use our mind as well as our heart in approaching relationships. Over a period of time, I added traits to my list until eventually I had forty-three items on it. Through the years, I have mentioned my list in various settings. Invariably, people laugh and make comments. But I contend that everyone has a list. It may not be written down, but everyone has a list. Would you date a smoker? Would you date someone who has custody of seven children? Would you date someone who has only a grade-school education? Would you date someone of a different race? Would you date someone of another faith, or of no specific faith? If you answered any of those questions easily, you have a list.

After I created my list, I took some more time to decide which items were essentials and which were just if-I-have-a-choice-why-not? On my current list there are only five essentials, and I'm considering relegating two of those to desirables. In one group where I talked about lists, a woman came up to me afterward and said that she definitely has a list, and she now dates only men whose mothers are dead or near death. She was partly joking, but only partly. Somewhere along the way, she had learned that men's relationships to their mothers have some bearing on their relationships with women in general, just as women's relationships to their fathers have some bearing on their relationships with men in general. The point in all this is the necessity of knowing ourselves and examining our needs. What do you need in relationships to help you be the best of who you are? Do you know? Are you aware of your needs? There's an old saying that if we aim at nothing we'll probably hit it. That's another way of saying that there are some things that we should not leave to chance—and I would add, to hormones.

After we make our list, it is helpful to look at the values that are represented by the items on it. One of my essentials in men is that they be people of genuine personal faith. The value behind this preference is my strong conviction that my faith is central to who I am as a person. Living all of life from a faith perspective is important to me. I make choices about how I spend my time, money, and energy that would make no sense to someone who does not understand and affirm the power of personal faith. A second essential is that the man have a commitment to a lifestyle of exercise and healthful eating. The value behind this for me is basic: I want to live. I have a terrible family history of heart disease and of diabetes, and if I am to live a long life with a good quality of life, I need to attend to those concerns. These two values—faith and personal lifestyle—affect choices I make every day of my life. If I were in a relationship with a man who did not share these values, our differing choices could strain the relationship and even destroy it. In relationships, differing values about daily things can become the grain of sand in a shoe that drives us crazy.

A few summers ago I needed to buy a dress for a family wedding. Knowing how difficult I am to fit (and how picky I am about clothes), I started months in advance looking for something appropriate. Several times I had stores to hold a dress for twenty-four hours so I could ask someone to come back with me to give a second opinion. I spent a long time looking for a dress. I knew in general what I wanted, but I was committed to looking until I found something that was just right. Compare that to our attitudes about finding someone for a significant friendship. I find it puzzling that we take great pains to find the right clothes or to match up the pieces of an outfit but leave things like relationships to chance. If we search for weeks to find a garment, why do we expect to find a significant other in the first group we encounter? It doesn't make much sense to approach life-shaping choices that way. Relationships are to be approached with care and with prayer.

If past relationships have not been what we wanted and needed them to be, we have to be willing to do things differently. If we do things the same as we always have, the outcomes will probably be the same as they have always been. One of my friends says that we "have to learn to turn off our radar." That is, some inner need or mechanism has guided us in the past to choose partners badly. So we have to learn not to give in to that inner pull. We have to choose not to respond to the kinds of people we've responded to in the past. We have to find a different way to look for relationships.

My model for good relationships goes back to the story of Eve and Adam. The first people were created with equality of value and equality of need. God made them partners in function, in caring for the earth and its animals, and God made them as partners for one another emotionally. Men and women need each other. In order to understand what it means to be human, we all need to know people of both sexes. We need to know all kinds of people to learn about all the many facets of being human. The left-brain types need to know right-brain types. Introverts need to know extroverts. Tidy people need to know slobs (and vice versa, though I'm not sure why). Numbers people need word people, and indoor people need outdoor people. Sports types need art types. We all need each other. If we shut ourselves off from relationships, we miss out on learning about the rich diversity that God made and in which I am sure God delights. God said of Adam that it was not good for him to be alone; God saw that people need each other. As Molly T. Marshall says in her book *What It Means to Be Human*, "Part of our shared work is to reflect the character of God on the earth. Neither male nor female can do this alone, but we can as interdependent creatures of God" as we live in community.[6] God made the first man and woman to live in a relationship where both were valued, where the needs of both were important, and God still intends that as our model. Mutual respect and honor are essential for healthy relationships.

I have come to see that my marriage never came close to being a relationship of mutual valuing and respect. My life revolved around my husband and getting his needs met, his wants attended to. Our household was as dysfunctional as any alcoholic family could have been, in the degree to which I made him the focus of all that went on. I made excuses for him (to myself as well as to others), I kept the secrets about our difficulties, I put aside my own needs. Getting and keeping him happy was the focus of our family. What I wanted and needed was unimportant; my pain and struggle were to be accepted. The fact that I was in pain did not justify changing our behavior. No matter what the cost to me as a person, we had to keep the relationship intact. But that was not a sustainable pattern.

Think about a business partnership. Suppose that one person contributed the capital, put in the long hours, and dealt with the personnel and customer-service hassles—but the other partner got all the income. We'd probably be able to see that such an arrangement was lopsided. We'd probably say it was doomed to eventual failure because a business that depends on one person is always vulnerable. If that one person becomes ill or for some other reason cannot function, the business cannot operate. But I could not see that my marriage was unbalanced. No wonder it failed when I could not go on. I crawled away, determined to stay clear of men for a while.

I made it for nine months. Then Charles came into our lives. I say "our" because it was my daughter who pulled us together. We met Charles at a singles event sponsored by our Sunday school class, and Emily fell in love. She thought he was wonderful. I didn't see it, but she has never looked to me before forming her opinions. The next Sunday after church, as we walked to the parking lot, she invited him to go to the park with us. We often went to the park on Sunday afternoons as a reward for good behavior because Emmy loved to play in the spray of the fountain there. I had not planned to invite him or anyone else to go along, but her spontaneous invitation was genuine. Charles looked at me, and I hesitantly nodded my agreement.

He was a quiet and deliberate man, very different than the hail-fellow-well-met ebullience that was Spence's way. Emmy's invitation put us in a situation where Charles could not hide, since there was only the three of us, and that allowed (forced) him to talk. He had always been single (I did not have anything about marital status on my list, though I assumed singleness). He worked as an accountant and was exploring, trying to find God's will for his life. (Being a person of faith was on my list.)

After a few weeks of friendly interaction in groups at singles events, Charles and I began dating. Within a month or so, I was beginning to think I was in love, and I soon told Charles that. With the calmness and care that I still love in him, he said, "Let's sit down. We need to talk." And he told me directly, so plainly that I could not possibly misunderstand, that it was too soon for me even to think about thinking I was in love. He said our goal should be to be friends and take our time. He enjoyed my company and I enjoyed his, and that was God's gift for this time in our lives. He said that I should be careful of any exclusive relationships for a while. I didn't want to hear that. I liked the easy, gentle companionship. He loved to do things around the house; he was great with Emmy; he was kind and funny and intelligent. He didn't talk much, but I quickly learned to listen to him when he did. He had a way of asking questions that went to the heart of any matter. Though his questions often made me squirm, they also caused me to stop and listen for God's voice. He was wonderful. Why shouldn't I fall in love with him? He was even short! (That's one of the desirables on my list.) The thought of being in love with him was enticing. But God protected me from myself in a remarkable way.

Just a few weeks after I made my I-think-I'm-falling-in-love-with-you declaration, a college acquaintance showed up at the singles class. He and I had known one another through a classmate who became his wife (and then his former wife). He was handsome, witty, outgoing, and ambitious. When he began paying attention to me, I was first astounded and then flattered. Then I was overwhelmed. He was delightful. When he asked me out, I was torn. I decided to do the only honest thing: I told him I'd been dating someone else, and I told Charles that someone else wanted to date me. Charles said he thought that was a good idea. He also said that he felt a bit jealous but that dating another man would be good for me. (See what a remarkable man he is?)

And so it was that I who thought I was so fat and ugly and stupid that no man would ever be interested in me found myself dating two wonderful men at the same time. We all attended singles functions, and I often found myself doing things with groups that included both of the guys. They respected and liked each other, and we got along well. Looking back now, I can see that it was a remarkable situation. I also believe that bringing two men into my life was God's grace at work protecting me from getting too deeply involved with any one person. I might have plunged ahead into a doomed second marriage if I had.

My friendships with these two men were both so radically different than any I had been in before that every interaction was an opportunity to learn. Charles respected me and listened to me and urged me to be myself. Richard stimulated me to think about things I'd never considered before. Both men had great senses of humor (though very different from one another), and we laughed a lot. Each of them treated me as an equal intellectually but more importantly, as an equal in value. When we discussed what to do or where to go, my opinion carried equal weight with theirs. When we talked about spiritual matters (which I did with both of them), they listened to me and accepted my ideas as valid. I was a real person, worth being with and worth accommodating.

These two wonderful men helped me to see how God wants us to honor one another, and I will always be grateful for their role in my life. They taught me how good relationships can be. Because of them, I was able to hope that I might actually be able to sustain healthy relationships. With them I discovered relationships characterized by mutual respect, fun, and support in growing in grace. Because of them, I will never settle for less again.

God made men and women to need each other, and when we search for good relationships, God works with us.

[1]Steven Callahan, *Adrift: Seventy-Six Days Lost at Sea* (Ballentine Books, Inc. 1989), Day 27.

[2]Bruce Fretts, "The Week," *Entertainment Weekly* (April 4, 1997): 3C.

[3]Joe Mandese. "How Much? Try a Million a Minute?" *Electronic Media* (September 16, 1996): 30.

[4]Ronald P. Philipchalk and James V. McConnell, *Understanding Human Behavior* 8th ed. (Fortworth, Tex.:Harcourt Brace College Publishers, 1994), 179–181.

[5]Stephanie Mansfield, "Bonding, Family Bonding," in *USA Weekend* (February 7-8, 1997): 7.

[6]Molly T. Marshall, *What It Means to Be Human* (Smyth and Helwys Publishing Company, Inc., 1995), 82.

CHAPTER 12

THIRTY-SEVEN GOING ON SEVENTEEN

If you were ever a teenager, you probably remember the awful insecurity. You wondered about how you looked and whether what you said was clever or just stupid and whether you ought to approach that person you were interested in and say something or just keep quiet and fade into the walls. It's just about the same to begin dating again as an adult. The title of this chapter comes from a book I read after my divorce—the title of which I've long since forgotten—whose author said that re-entering the dating process after marriage made him feel like he was a teenager again. Those words have stuck in my mind all these years because they seemed so apt. The big difference, of course, is that we're not teenagers. We don't look like it, and we can't get away with acting like it.

The years that have passed have changed us, and the world has changed too. Dating customs and behaviors have changed. It seems silly to call a fifty-year-old man a BOYfriend, just as it seems silly to think of myself as a GIRLfriend. It's been years since I could call myself a girl and keep a straight face. Many other things have changed too. Women call men for dates. Men and women take turns paying for dinner or entertainment. Many unmarried couples travel together and no one seems to notice or care. Hard-driving professional people apply their managerial skills to the problem of finding a partner just as they would any other challenge. Paid matchmaking services are not just for musical comedies; people actually use them. I get mailings from one here in town regularly, and I have a friend who last year married a man she found through one of them. Things have definitely changed.

But one thing that has not changed is our need and hunger for love, affirmation, and companionship. We continue to search for fulfilling friendships. Are there rules for us to follow? It would be nice if there were a list of commandments ("Thou shalt not date anyone who was a friend of thee and thy former spouse; thou shalt not kiss on a first date; thou shalt not lie about the existence of thy children; thou shalt not date for one year after thy spouse's death (or the granting of thy divorce decree); thou shalt not . . .). At least then we would have a common basis for discussion. But there are no rules for the way dating is done these days. (Actually, there is a book called *The Rules*, but it advocates women lying about former marriages and children, and using various kinds of manipulation to "catch" a man. I like to remind people that fish in a lake don't want to be "caught" because of what happens next.)

It seems to me that people of faith expect more of themselves and their companions than the culture at large asks. I have talked with many believers who seek ways to approach dating relationships that honor our partners and our commitment to Christ. That can be difficult. As the story of Adam and Eve shows, men and women are created to live together and to serve God together. Unfortunately, we do not always have a clear picture of what that means and how we are to go about finding companions. Many ideas that we hear over and over limit rather than help us in the search. For example, some of us have been taught that there is one right person "out there" for us. We look for the one person who will be our complement, whom we can love perfectly and fit with in every way. This idea reminds me of an ancient myth that explains the relationship and origin of the sexes. The story (the voice of Aristophanes in Plato's *Symposium* from the *Dialogues of Plato*)[1] tells about creatures that encompass all human attributes and possibilities. They displease the gods and as punishment are cleft into two beings, one male and one female, and separated. They are doomed to roam the earth, eternally seeking their other half so they can be complete again.

Vestiges of this "searching for the one right person" who is our other half idea color many of our interactions. I know I struggled with trying to discern which of the two men I was dating was the better match for me. The fact that I loved both of them was confusing. Both were good Christians. If I loved each of them and saw good in each of them, why should I dismiss either of them? And yet much of my conditioning led me to believe that one or the other of them could not be God's choice for me, since God had one specific man for me—if I could just find him. I had no reason to end the relationship with either of these two.

Ideas about female and male as two different sides of humanity (and even of individual personalities, as in Jung's theories) may influence us to see people of the other sex as wholly "other," unlike us and yet necessary to our lives. In leading retreats for singles and talking with them about their attitudes toward relationships, I have discovered that some people see those of the opposite sex primarily as possible mates. I first encountered this idea in my college roommate. I worked in the college library, and one night I had a fascinating conversation with a man who was doing some research. I told my roommate about him when I returned to our room, and she asked, "Is he married?"

"I don't know. That didn't come up in the conversation."

"Oh come on! Didn't you look at his left hand? That's the first thing I do when I meet a guy."

"You're kidding! You don't really do that, do you? Why?"

"Because if he's married, I don't need to get to know him. He's not available."

For her, males were first and foremost potential mates. Some people stay away from singles groups because they believe they will encounter this attitude in all the people there. It's true that many people come to singles groups to find potential dates. Some people come to find their next spouse, and they make no bones about it. The aura of near desperation that some people exude makes it clear that they are waiting to latch on to someone. Sizing up people primarily as "the opposite sex" creates a barrier to the quality of friendship and interaction that I believe God wants for us.

People are not always aware of these attitudes or give much thought to where they come from. Over the years I've thought a lot about this and talked to a number of people, and I think it may have to do with the setting in which people grow up. I have always had guys for friends, and some guys have female friends with whom there is no overtone of romance. I don't see men first as potential mates, and I wonder if that comes from growing up with brothers. Males are not wholly "other" to me, mysterious creatures with whom I must work to connect; they are people who happen to be male.

When I have asked in groups whether people have platonic friendships with people of the opposite sex, almost always the people who do are those who grew up in a mixed-sex environment. People who have lived with siblings of the opposite sex or had close friendships with cousins or even neighbors of the opposite sex seem more able to see men and women as varieties of the same general kind of creature. Many women who grew up living only with girls and many men who grew up living only with boys seem to view people of the opposite sex as "other," as possible mates, rather than simply as people. Such utilitarian attitudes can reduce our interactions with others to mere shopping excursions.

If we approach others with a prospector's gleam in our eyes, they will sense our motives. People want to be valued for who they are as individuals, not for what they can do for us. Paul wrote to the Galatians, "There is no longer male and female; for all of you are one in Christ Jesus" (Gal. 3:28). Believers are to receive and honor one another not on the basis of sex but as co-heirs with Christ. Male or female, every person we meet deserves our respect and consideration as one for whom Christ died. That applies to the people we date just as it does to all others. One of the great benefits of participating in singles groups can be making friendships with both men and women. In an environment of shared faith, we can talk together about our lives and learn to know one another as people first. For me, talking with men in our singles group helped me to work through my feelings about my divorce. They also helped me to understand Spencer's possible feelings (and therefore helped me in my work on forgiveness).

However, as I listened to both men and women talk about the pain and loss they were feeling, I was able to see that we were all very much the same. We harbored the same hopes and fears, and we hurt in the same ways. Knowing that helped me to approach others carefully.

Eventually, I felt I was ready to begin dating again. But being Christian and dating Christian men did not make relationships easy. One struggle I was not prepared for was the struggle about sexual issues. When I divorced, I did so with a commitment to celibacy. I believed that my faith required this of me. What I did not understand was how difficult it would be. During the years of my marriage, I had become accustomed to sexual expression as a part of my relationship with my husband. My church's official statement affirms sexuality as "God's good gift" to us, and I had experienced sex as a good part of marriage. I had been married for several years, and during that time I had come to see sex as a natural part of a close relationship with my husband. After my divorce, when I felt affection and warmth toward the men I was dating, sexual desire was a part of that.

What helped me and the men I dated was knowing where we stood on this issue. Charles and I shared a commitment to celibacy. We were honest with each other about what we felt God wanted and about how difficult it was to live by that standard. I remain grateful to this day for the openness of our discussions. Because we had voiced our commitments, when passion flared one or the other of us could cool things down by reminding the other of them. I was not always the strong one, and he was not always the strong one—but we were able to protect each other. I remember one night when Charles suddenly stopped kissing me, stood up, and said, "I have to go now." He strode across the room, put on his jacket, quickly walked out, and said goodnight to me through the screen door. On another occasion, I said to him, "Going further would be wonderful, I know, but we can't do that. That would not be what God wants for us." He agreed, and we said goodnight. As he said to me on one occasion, sex would be not be bad; it would be good—but good can be the opposite of best. God's best for us was what we both wanted. Part of being an adult means realizing what you're missing—and deciding that it's better to do without it than to make an error that would harm both persons in the relationship.

That was really the heart of our being able to resist giving in to our passion: we cared about one another and about helping one another live by what we believed. Charles was a man of such faith and deep integrity that I knew breaking his commitment would cause him great anguish later. Though I often wanted more than we had, I would find myself thinking of him. He would feel terrible, and I did not want him to have to endure that. Knowing his standards and the man he was, I wanted to protect him. He was able to do the same for me.

Our relationship taught me how important shared values and honesty are. We had been completely honest about what we wanted and about what we believed, and we respected each other's ideals. Though I was not consciously aware of it at the time, we were living by what Paul told the Romans. Chapter 14 of the Epistle to the Romans is a discussion of what is permissible for believers and what is not and about respecting and honoring differing standards.

The Roman Christians were arguing about rules of personal conduct. Some believers thought it was wrong to buy meat that came from temple sacrifices. These temples to various Roman deities had ceremonies in which animals were slaughtered. The meat not used in the offerings was then taken to the market to be sold. Some Christians would not buy or eat this meat and felt that those who did so were sinning. Other believers said that there was nothing wrong with eating this meat if it was received with thanksgiving to God (Rom. 15:1). But Paul urged the believers to consider one another's scruples, saying, "Those who eat must not despise those who abstain, and those who abstain must not pass judgment on those who eat" (Rom. 14:3).

Another issue was observance of holy days. Some believers kept many Sabbath rules, while others believed that Christ had released them from any obligation to keep the Jewish laws about it. They were also arguing about whether or not it was acceptable to drink wine. In all these matters, Paul said, people were to follow their own conscience as they were "fully convinced in their own minds" (14:5). He told the Romans, "We do not live to ourselves, and we do not die to ourselves" but to the Lord, and it is to the Lord—not to one another—that we will answer. Paul believed that "nothing is unclean in itself." Those who could eat the meat with a clear conscience were free to do so. But he also told the strong believers—those who kept fewer rules—that it is wrong for us to "make others fall." We are not to "do anything that makes [a] brother or sister stumble," (Rom. 14:7,14, 20) so if someone else's faith would be shaken by what we allow, we are to consider that person before we act. This advice has obvious applications in dating relationships.

It is inevitable that questions about the limits of sexual expression will become part of romantic relationships. I feel sure that others who have been absolutely faithful in marriage will find as I did that self-control is not as clear an issue after marriage as it was in our virginal days. Deep affection toward a person of the opposite sex will probably lead to stirrings of sexual desire, and we must confront the issues honestly.

Questions of sexuality are emotionally charged ones for most of us. No matter what we were taught, these issues tap into deep feelings. For those whose spouses were unfaithful during marriage, questions about sexuality after marriage are often still mixed with feelings of anger and betrayal. Added to that, many people who were completely monogamous may find themselves bewildered by attraction not just to one person but to several. At first I wondered how people of integrity could be so pulled by hormones. But I have come to see that integrity doesn't counteract hormones any more than a desire to eat healthy foods cancels out the fat and calories in cheesecake.

I found it less than helpful for married friends to give me advice about what I ought and ought not do. It is easy for married people to say, "Go home and take a cold shower and put sex out of your mind" when they can go home and snuggle with a beloved partner. Their attempts to help did nothing to make my yearnings go away; they only made me feel guilty for being so tempted. And yet I wanted to honor God in this area of my life.

The only way for us to do that is to seek what Paul described, a place where we are "fully convinced in [our] own minds," so that we have a clear sense of who we are as God's children. But that is not always easy to do. I had to find a way to separate what I thought and believed from what others were telling me—on both sides of the issue.

We tend to blend our cultural ideas with Bible stories in ways that make it difficult to separate what we have heard from what the Bible actually says. As we were talking about divorce in our Sunday school class one day, a woman said, "But doesn't the Bible say we're to stay together 'until death do us part'?" The biblical model in the Hebrew scriptures is the man taking the woman into his tent or him coming into hers. In the New Testament, there's the wedding in Cana of Galilee (John 2:1-11)—which was a really big party with lots of wine and no mention of vows. There are some other wedding feasts mentioned, but there's nothing in the stories about wedding ceremonies or vows. We've just heard the vows so many times in church that we assume they come from the Bible.

We dwell on and repeat what we think the Bible says, without looking carefully at the actual stories. The knight in shining armor and pristine princess are not embodiments of biblical ideals. In the Bible, women were given as prizes in war (Saul's daughter, 1 Sam. 18:20-25, 27) and handed from one man to another (Samson's first wife, Judges 14:20). Lot offered his daughters as sexual playthings to the men at his door, saying, "I have two daughters who have not known a man; let me bring them out to you, and do to them as you please" (Gen. 19:8). Men had multiple wives; this was so common that the Law contained rules requiring men to treat unloved wives equally with loved ones (Deut. 21:15-17). There's a lot we think the Bible says that is difficult to find there. The Bible does not directly address many of the situations in which single adults find themselves.

Even if we could establish clear rules, however, these are not ends in themselves. When we teach children to look both ways before crossing the street, we do so in order to protect them. They may comply at first only because we say so. But our hope is that children will mature and eventually learn to look both ways not just because someone says so but because they understand the danger and want to take care of themselves. The same is true for rules about our behavior as adults. Maturity is getting beyond "because I said so" or because anybody says so in keeping the rules. We make our standards our own, a part of who we are, in order to care for ourselves and do what we know is best for ourselves and others. We internalize our standards to the point that they guide our behavior. We don't have to struggle with each situation as a completely new challenge and we feel no need to explain or justify. We can simply state who we are. Some people don't believe anyone is celibate; some are shocked that everyone isn't. Either way, we still answer individually for our behavior.

It is easy to see why we want people to control their sexual impulses. Sexual drives are powerful, and we fear what people will do. Anyone who has ever lived with teenagers knows how powerful and disconcerting sexual energy can be. My neighbor, mother of several sons, once said that teenage boys are hormones with feet. This idea is not foreign to the Bible. It shows both men and women to be lusty creatures, and as the Book of Proverbs says over and over, sexual desire can be a trap that leads to great trouble. Because sexual drives are so strong, we almost fear our sexuality. But if we date, we must face our needs and make Bible-based decisions as to how we are going to conduct ourselves. Only by doing so can we enter into relationships honestly and openly.

Though I do not think the Bible directly addresses many of the questions we face as singles, it does offer us guidance. Many of the New Testament epistles tell us to live lives that are above reproach, that those around us may be drawn to God. First Corinthians 6 reminds us that our bodies are God's temple and that we are to honor God in what we do with our bodies. As I said earlier, Romans tells us to respect one another's standards and to support one another in living our faith as we believe we are to live it. Matthew 5:8 says that the "pure in heart . . . will see God," implying that not being pure in heart will interfere with our seeing God. If we are to feel "pure in heart," we must live as we feel God calls us to live. Doing anything less will interfere with our relationship with God.

What does this mean in practical terms? How do we apply these ideas day by day? For me, it has meant working to be clear in my own mind about my needs and about my standards. The first difficulty can be identifying what I need. The lines between sexual needs and other needs are often blurred. In Maslow's hierarchy, the most basic level of need is the need for survival, both personally and as a species. This includes the need to reproduce, which is clearly linked with sexuality. However, for many of us the need for love and belongingness includes being affirmed as sexually desirable too. The need for social status and power often includes being seen with the "right" people, including the right escort, which also touches on our sexual identity and sexual needs. Advertising uses promises of sexual attractiveness and conquest to sell everything from cars to toothpaste, so I can understand why I sometimes am not sure of the origin of what I'm feeling. At any given moment, do I want someone to love me for who I am, or do I just want the status of having a date on Saturday night? Am I yearning for companionship, or do I merely want to be sure people see me at this party?

This confusion of sexuality with self-worth comes through in many ways. In *Bull Durham* the character Annie (portrayed by Susan Sarandon) talks about her sexual liaisons with various ball players. In reflecting on these relationships, she says, "I make them feel confident, and they make me feel safe . . . and pretty." Like Annie, sometimes what I need is affirmation of my attractiveness; but it is possible to separate that need from having sex.

If we do not take time to be aware of our true needs, we may use the wrong means to get them met and in the process, use other people as well. First Thessalonians 4:3-6 tells us clearly that we are not to exploit one another sexually in order to get our needs met. When I find myself yearning for male companionship, I ask myself what I am really wanting. Sometimes I need to be held; sometimes I need emotional intimacy, the feeling of being known deeply and accepted as I am by another person. If I am unclear about what I need, I may mislead my partner into thinking I am seeking sex when what I really want is a hug or a long talk. If I am to be fair to the men I date, I owe it to them to know my own needs and to be honest about them.

Honesty is a big deal with me, and I look for it in the men I date. When I began going out with the man I am dating now, we talked about our goals for relationships. He said, "What about marriage? Do you want to get married?" I was glad to get this part of the relationship out in the open.

"I'm not opposed to marriage, but I'm also not eager to be married. If I met someone and fell in love and he wanted to get married, I'd consider it. But I'm comfortable being single. I like it." That is the way I feel.

The other day I got a flyer from a local matchmaking service that calls itself "the dignified alternative to the singles scene." The "preliminary profile" they asked me to return had three choices under "My primary social goal is." The choices were "To date a lot," "To have a steady relationship" and "Marriage."(3) I applaud that level of directness and recommend it. It may limit us, but that is better than what happens in some cases.

Sometimes knowing and even expressing our needs is not enough. I have a friend, a man, whom I have known for about eight or nine years. He dates a lot. From the time I met him, he has been clear that he does not want to date women who have young children at home, much less marry one. He would not get into steady relationships with women who had children. Then he met a woman whom he really liked, who also had children at home. They dated for quite a while—well over a year—and eventually she gave him an ultimatum: marry me or the relationship is over. He walked away from the relationship, and she was furious. Tales of his awful behavior began circulating in our singles group, and finally I talked with her over breakfast about the end of their relationship. As I suspected, he had told her clearly that he did not want to assume parenting duties. I asked her if she had known his feelings from the beginning. She said she had. I asked her if he had misled her in any way during the relationship to make her think he had changed his mind or that he intended to marry her. She thought about it, and finally said, "No, he did not." I wanted to shake her. Like many I have seen, she thought she could change his mind.

People like me and that man often find that people don't believe us when we say we don't intend to be married. Over and over, I have seen people who want to get married get into relationships with partners who say quite openly that they intend to remain single. The person who wants to marry either keeps that desire a secret or says it's okay that the other doesn't want to marry. But then they set out to change the other person's mind. They believe that they can love the person so much and be such a perfect partner that the other will want to marry. Eventually they deliver an ultimatum like my friend received. Then, when the unwilling partner leaves, the giver of the ultimatum acts like the injured party. The scenario reminds me of a cartoon I saw. A horse is standing at a fence talking with a cow, saying, "All my life I've been a horse. Don't expect me to change now." Believing that we can change someone into what we want is a recipe for disappointment and hurt.

We can avoid hurt (and wasted time, if you're one of those whose five-year plan includes remarrying) by knowing what we want and need before we enter relationships. As with the question of whether we want to marry, if your standard is celibacy, it is important to make that clear to potential partners. That will mean that some people will choose not to date you, but you will also avoid the arguments and the hurt of having to say good-bye later to someone you have grown to care for deeply.

I wish I could say that being clear about your standard will also allow you to avoid being pressured to have sex, but some people think they can change others' minds about that, too, just as about marriage. The standard of Romans 14 is clear, though: we sin if we push others to go against what they believe God asks of them. The standard in any relationship must be to follow the conscience of the partner who allows less freedom. We can remind one another of our commitments in loving ways and help one another to be our best selves.

In an admittedly unscientific effort, I have been collecting information from Christian singles about what they look for in potential partners. In church gatherings and on retreats, I have distributed forms for people to list the traits or characteristics they seek in a romantic partner. The quality listed most frequently by both men and women is that a good partner must be a person of faith. This is not a big surprise, since the groups were Christian groups; 80% of women listed being Christian as a trait they seek, and 41% of men listed that. The next two traits that women seek in men are a sense of humor and being college-educated (tied in frequency). The fourth most frequently listed trait (by women) is honesty/trustworthiness.

Men also listed a sense of humor second most frequently as a trait they seek in partners. Being well-educated and not being overweight tied for third place for preferences among men, but if the traits of being well-educated and intelligent are combined, that would be the number-one trait men look for. However, 65% of the men who filled out forms mentioned some physical attribute they seek in a woman. Physical traits are clearly important to men, but the traits they listed were not the same ones. About 25% of the men listed "physically attractive" as a general trait they seek; another 25% listed not being overweight; another 15% listed some specific physical trait such as being tall, short, or brunette. If these responses had been counted in a general category "physical attributes," that would have been the most common response given by men. To be fair, it is important to note that 22% of women listed "physically attractive" or some other specific trait they seek in men. "Physically fit," which may be a politically correct way of saying "not overweight" when describing men, was listed by another 25%. If these two categories are combined as with the physical attributes listed by men, almost half of women count physical attributes as important. The women who have returned surveys are not really all that different from men in noticing and valuing appearance.

What does all this say to us about seeking partners? It tells us at least that some of us know what we want. Taking the time to reflect on what we want and need in a partner is the first step toward finding it. Both men and women see the value of shared faith, a sense of humor, and intelligence. That gives us a lot of common ground with many of the people we meet, if these groups have been representative. There are many different sets of preferences; respondents to my surveys have listed nearly one hundred different traits that they value. This should encourage us, because each of us has traits that others seek in relationships. Paul's description of the Body of Christ in 1 Corinthians 12 tells us that God has designed us to be different from one another and that in the body of Christ there is a place for all different kinds of people. In the enormous variety of God's people, we can be encouraged that whatever we seek in a partner, there is probably someone out there who shares our faith and is looking for what we have to offer.

What is most important to remember about relationships is that what we do within them matters to God. Every part of life is an arena for discipleship; every relationship is an opportunity to honor God and to live out our faith.

---

[1] *The Dialogues of Plato*, ed. B. Jowett (New York: Random House, 1937). Quoted in Judith Pintar, *The Halved Soul: Retelling the Myths of Romantic Love.* (London: Pandora Press, 1992), pp. 15-16.

CHAPTER 13

FLYING SOLO

S *unstone* magazine printed a tongue-in-cheek "Top Ten Biblical Ways to Acquire/Get a Wife."

Here they are:

10) Find an attractive prisoner of war, bring her home, shave her head, trim her nails, and give her new clothes. Then she's yours. (Deut. 21:11-13)

9) Find a prostitute, and marry her. (Hosea 1:1-3)

8) Go to a party, and hide. When the women come out to dance, grab one and carry her off to be your wife. —Benjaminites (Judg. 21:19-25)

7) Cut 200 foreskins off your future father-in-law's enemies, and get his daughter for a wife. —David (1 Sam. 18:27)

6) Become the emperor of a huge nation and hold a beauty contest. —Xerxes or Ahasuerus (Esther 2:3-4)

5) When you see someone you like, go home and tell your parents, "I have seen a ... woman; now get her for me."—Samson (Judges 14:1-3)

4) Kill any husband, and take HIS wife (prepare to lose four sons, though). —David (2 Sam. 11)

3) Wait for your brother to die. Take his widow. (It's not just a good idea; it's the law.) (Deut. 25:5-10)

2) Don't be so picky. Make up for quality with quantity. (1 Kings 11:1-3)

1) *And the number one biblical way to acquire a wife is ...* "A wife? ... Are you kidding me?" —Paul (1 Cor. 7:32-35)

To be fair to the female 50.4% of earth's population, I came up with a companion list, "Ten Biblical Ways to Acquire/Get a Husband." Here they are:

10) Ask God to send an angel to convince the man to marry you. (Matt. 1:18-24)

9) Have your father slip you into a man's tent after dark on his wedding night and keep your identity secret until it's too late for the young man to object. (Gen. 29:13-27)

8) Offer to water his servant's camels. (Gen. 24:1-58)

7) Get your dad to fix you up with one of his employees. (Exod. 2:15-21)

6) Have your former in-laws fix you up with your ex-husband's best man. (Judges 14:1-20)

5) Trick your former father-in-law into having sex with you, get pregnant, and pressure him to do the honorable thing. (Gen. 38)

4) Go to a party, and, after the man has eaten and drunk and fallen asleep, crawl into bed with him; then when he wakes up, remind him to do right by you. (Ruth 3:1-14)

3) Bathe nude within sight of your neighbors (but only if you're beautiful, of course). (2 Sam. 11)

2) Ask God to make you one from scratch. (Gen. 1:26-27)

1) And the number one biblical way to acquire a husband is . . . "A husband? Are you kidding me?" (1 Cor. 7:32-35)

These tongue-in-cheek lists make light of some unusual Bible incidents that tell how people found mates. Of course, we think that we and other modern people would never do any of those things. They seem extreme.

But though our methods vary from those in the lists, we do seem interested in finding mates. I went to a Christian bookstore the other day to check out the titles in the "Singles" section. There were several books on how to build a singles program in the church. There were also four others: *Lady in Waiting: Developing Your Love Relationships, Knight in Shining Armor, Discovering Your Lifelong Love,* and *51 Good Things To Do While You're Waiting for the Right One to Come Along.*

Among those titles, there were none about discovering God's call for us as single people. So I went to an on-line bookstore on the world-wide web. Of the Christian books on singleness, 10 out of a total of 586 supported singles in being single. Many titles seem to indicate that those who are single are just in a holding pattern, waiting for marriage.

Though marriage is a dream many people cherish, not all single people want to be married. In fact, I meet more and more single people who are very clear that marriage is not for them. Like me, they have discovered that the single life offers great rewards and great opportunities. It can be a wonderful and fulfilling way to live.

In the first years after my divorce, I read everything I could find on Christians and divorce—theology, personal experience, singles' program handbooks, divorce recovery workbooks. After a while I recognized a definite pattern in the personal-experience books. They tell of the author's struggle to recover from grief and loss and build a new life. The writer learns some important spiritual lessons—and then meets a wonderful Christian person and remarries. (I remember only one exception, Jason Towner's book, *Jason Loves Jane But They Got a Divorce*.) It may not have been intentional, but the message seemed to be that the sign a person is healed and "normal" again is remarriage.

After my sabbatical from romantic relationships following my divorce, I had a short bout with want-to-get-married-again-itis. But as I said in an earlier chapter, God protected me by sending two men into my life. Over the next year, as I continued to date and love them both, it became clear that I was approaching a point where I was going to have to choose between them. As I was thinking and praying about my dilemma, asking God for direction, I was offered a job in another city. So I took the easy path: I got out of Dodge—I left both of the men and moved several hundred miles away. It took me a while to see what was probably obvious to others: if deep in my heart I wanted to marry, why did I leave? The answer, of course, was that I wasn't really sure that I wanted to remarry. My inability to think about a permanent commitment to either of the good men in my life was evidence that I was not ready to marry. And for several years after I moved, I was too busy with my job and my child to have time or energy for a relationship.

One morning several years ago as I was getting ready for work, I was looking for something that I do not use often. Standing at the vanity sink in my bedroom, I opened the drawer on the left and rifled through it. Couldn't find what I needed. I opened the drawer on the right and looked there. Couldn't find it there, either. I opened in turn each of the doors below the sink, and finally went back to the drawer on the left. As I looked down at the crowded drawer, I thought to myself, "Look at this! Every drawer, every space, is crammed full. It's obvious I could never marry again—there's no room here for anyone else!" I smiled, but that half-joking comment from me to me became an image for my life. It is very full, with many good things. Relationships are an important part of that fullness, but marriage is not one of the relationships. For this time in my life and for the foreseeable future, I am essentially a single person. And there are many people like me.

Though I don't see eye to eye with the Apostle Paul on many things, I agree with him on this: some people are called to be single. In chapter 7 of his First Epistle to the Corinthians, Paul writes at length about whether or not believers ought to marry. He says that remaining single is preferable to being married. This was a revolutionary idea in Paul's time. The Jewish standard was marriage and children, but choosing celibacy caught on in Christian circles in the early years of the church. It was such a success, in fact, that one scholar says choosing celibacy over marriage "eventually became the most striking contrast between Judaism and Christianity."[1] Many early believers chose a life of singleness and service.

The most familiar model most of us have for this calling is priests and lay brothers (monks) and sisters (nuns) in the Roman Catholic church. Protestant models also exist. I have a friend who became an Episcopalian nun, and I visit a retreat center that until a few years ago was operated by Protestant sisterhood whose convent still stands on the grounds. But these groups are not highly visible; in fact, many people do not know that there is such a thing as a Protestant nun. In the Protestant church, religious groups such as the Shakers and others where few or none of the members marry have been curiosities if not oddities.

But Paul makes it clear a life of singleness is not for everyone, saying, "I wish that all were as I myself am. But each has a particular gift from God" (1 Cor.7:7) and goes on to tell the Corinthians that each of them is to live the life "to which God called you" (1 Cor. 7:17). The key, of course, is discerning God's call, and frankly there is not a great deal of support for discovering whether we are meant to remain single. Some families make it clear that adult children are expected to produce grandchildren according to a fairly specific schedule, and marriage is assumed as a prerequisite for that. People don't examine whether marriage is right for them.

Even after divorce, some people don't take time to consider whether part of their difficulty with marriage might be that they are not suited for it. They may move quickly into another relationship. One of the characters in the movie *Forget Paris* does just that. Later, talking unhappily to a friend about her marriages, she says, "If I took time before or between [relationships], you know, to find out who I really am, by myself, who I could be, you know, without any guy around." Many of us don't take time to find out who we really are in relationship to other people and even to God.

Singleness for many people is, in writer Susan Annette Muto's words, "neither fully appraised nor freely chosen."[2] This is true in several ways. Several years ago in her excellent book *Celebrating the Single Life*, Muto wrote about those in her Roman Catholic tradition who enter into religious life and find that it is not right for them. Because a call to religious life is considered the highest call, Muto says some Roman Catholic families may subtly pressure sons and daughters to enter the priesthood or the convent. These people may find themselves unfitted for religious life and, after much soul searching, discover that what they thought were their own choices were not, that the single life was not "freely chosen." They discover that the dream is the family's dream, not theirs. Not "freely chosen" can be true in another way for those of us who find ourselves single again. We may not want to be single, we may not have chosen it, but nevertheless we are single. And the Apostle Paul saw this as on opportunity. He told the Corinthians that those who found themselves unmarried or widowed would do well to remain so.

Whether we planned to be single or find ourselves surprised to be single, Paul's words invite us to self-examination. We owe it to ourselves and to God to examine our situation, to listen for God's call. Muto says that being single offers opportunity to "live in tune with reality in a more reflective way." Remaining free of marriage may allow us to take advantage of opportunities for ministry and for personal spiritual growth that would be difficult to pursue otherwise. Several years ago I participated in an intensive spiritual-formation program that spanned two years. It required a great deal of reading, a personal project, lifestyle changes, personal spiritual disciplines, and one week in residence with other participants each quarter. I was free to pursue that opportunity with no guilt or stress on a relationship with a spouse. When I want to make a spiritual retreat or am invited to lead one, I am free to make that decision without having to consult anyone. I enjoy that freedom.

It is easy to think, as actress Rene Russo said, that having a mate will make our lives complete and make us happy. But if we are unhappy single, we'll be unhappy married. It's not marriage or singleness that makes happiness; happiness is the product of loving God and oneself and being free to love others. I felt like half a person in many ways after my divorce, and I sought counseling to help me discover why. One of the books I read was *One Is a Whole Number*. Through it I came to see wholeness as God's offer to each of us, whether or not we are married. We can be whole even if we are not perfect and healed in every way, and our wholeness is personal, not a part of marriage. Becoming whole is something we do for ourselves, as a foundation for all healthy relationships—whether or not we ever marry.

This does not mean that we should deny our resistance to being single, however. Discomfort with being single and yearnings that won't go away can be God calling us to go deeper. We discover our own needs and God's work within us as we spend time reading, thinking, and waiting in God's presence. I believe, as Proverbs 20:27 says, "The human spirit is the lamp of the Lord," so I pay attention to my emotions and yearnings. God uses them to draw me closer, to shed light on my way and to guide me in examining my motives and my needs.

Some needs are especially salient for some single people. In writing to the Corinthians, Paul says that sexual needs may make it advisable for some people to marry. But awareness of and struggling with sexual needs should not lead us to conclude that we are called to marriage rather than singleness. To some extent it is necessary to separate sexual yearnings from the question of whether we are called to singleness. Think of it this way: getting married does not end sexual temptation. Marriage provides an outlet for sexual expression, but that does not mean that married people are never tempted. Marriage means making a commitment to another person to prefer that one above all others and to not act on our sexual attraction to others. Faithfulness is a choice that people make over and over again. In a similar way, a call to singleness does not mean that we will never have to deal with sexual needs or sexual temptation.

I read a story about this recently that gave me a new appreciation for the strength of sexual attraction and the need for vigilance. The story was about David DuPlessis, a legendary and beloved leader in the holiness movement. He was known for his purity of life and fidelity; he was a man above reproach. A few years before Dr. DuPlessis's death, a young man came to him and said, "I'm committed to serving Jesus Christ with my whole heart and to living in purity—body, soul and mind. Still, I sometimes have struggles with my thought life. Could you tell me, sir, about how old I'll be when improper thoughts—especially about women—won't tempt my mind any longer?"

Dr. DuPlessis, then seventy-nine years old, said, "Son, when I get that old, I'll let you know!"[3] This godly man was also honest and funny.

A commitment to follow God in either marriage or singleness does not mean that sexual struggles will end. I heard someone say once that Eastern thought teaches that greater spiritual awareness brings heightened awareness in all areas of life and may heighten sexual drives. By the same token, low libido and lack of awareness of sexual needs cannot be equated with a call to singleness. Sexual needs are a normal part of life, and being fully aware of our sexuality is part of being whole and healthy people. Choosing to remain single simply means that we will have a different struggle with these needs than married people do. All of us are called to honor God in how we handle our sexual needs, whether we are married or single.

After saying that either remaining single or marrying is acceptable, Paul goes on to make the statements that are the basis of the number-one items on the "Top Ten Biblical Ways . . ." lists: "The unmarried man is anxious about the affairs of the Lord, how to please the Lord; but the married man is anxious about the affairs of the world, how to please his wife, and his interests are divided. And the unmarried woman and the virgin are anxious about the affairs of the Lord, so that they may be holy in body and in spirit; but the married woman is anxious about the affairs of the world, how to please her husband" (1 Cor. 7:32-34). These words make clear the issue for Paul: remaining single allows us to give more of our attention to God. He tells the Corinthians that his advice is meant "to promote . . . unhindered devotion to the Lord" (v. 35).

Think about that for a moment. What hinders devotion to the Lord? I know that bad relationships have at times hindered my spiritual growth and interfered with my obedience to God. During the years I struggled to save my marriage, I was often of little use to God in any form of ministry. I had no energy to care for others or to reach out to them. Another way that relationships can hinder our devotion is by keeping us from discovering who we are "alone . . . without any" romantic interest around.

Sometimes in relationships we change in order to please the other person, perhaps without even realizing it. Someone we're dating makes a comment about liking a particular hairstyle or a particular color of clothing, and we are influenced by that comment the next time we consider changing our hairstyle or buying a new garment. Or we change the way we spend our time, doing things we don't really enjoy because the other person likes them. How many of us have boxes of unused stuff that we accumulated when we were dating the person who enjoyed hiking or ice skating or classical music or backgammon? In subtle and not-so-subtle ways, we change in order to please others. To again quote Deborah Winger's character in *Forget Paris*, we may find that we are "constantly reinventing [ourselves] in order to be the perfect person" for that relationship. When this is the case, we may find it difficult to know who we are—and this makes it difficult to offer to God all that we are. Part of our worship is to stand honestly before God, naming both our strengths and our weaknesses, for in our uniqueness each of us offers God unique worship. If we do not worship God as we are, with all that we are, God will be missing out on something that only we can give. As part of our "unhindered devotion," we explore who we are in order to serve God with all that we have to give. Knowing ourselves allows us to know God more honestly and fully. As John Calvin said in the Institutes of the Christian Religion, "without knowledge of self there is no knowledge of God."

I learned some surprising things about myself in the months and years following my marriage. One of my surprises was finding out that I need time alone. I had never been alone much until my divorce. The first several times Emily went to stay with her father, I was very lonely. I was uncomfortable being in the house alone. It wasn't fear; it was the strangeness. But eventually I found myself irritable if Emily missed several times with her father, and I realized it was because I was missing my time alone. The solitude gave me time to read, to write, to pray, to do nothing with no one pulling on me for anything. Having this special time to take care of myself helped me to act on my determination to love myself, and as I consciously did that, I found that I was more able to feel God's love for me. In these times with no distractions and no demands, I enjoyed an openness and intimacy with God that made me long for more of the same. Spending time alone with God was and is balm for my soul, and when I am feeling tattered and used up, solitude restores me. It took me a long time to discover that.

You may have heard the saying, "Don't speak unless doing so will improve upon the silence." Susan Muto says a corollary of that is, "Don't be with people unless doing so improves upon the solitude." That can help in making decisions about whether to go places and do things. Having the opportunity to be alone is a wonderful part of the single life. My dear mother-in-law used to say, "I just love being by myself! I'm in such good company, don't you know!" I came to understand exactly what she meant.

I learned other things about myself too. I learned that I can replace the heating element in an oven and that I can caulk bathrooms, paint, and do maintenance chores around the house. I can talk intelligently with a mechanic and get my car repaired (and re-repaired until it's right). I can make decisions about changing jobs. I can understand pension plans and buy and sell a house (and do all the tax forms that accompany those transactions). And perhaps most important, I can say no to things that are not right for me to do, things that don't fit in with who I am or who God is calling me to be.

We can't tell others who they are meant to be, and others cannot tell us who we are meant to be. Discovering God's call to us as individuals is a personal search. However, there are some personal characteristics that undergird the single life, and, as Susan Muto says, "Grace builds on nature." Our inborn traits and preferences become the basis on which God builds us and through which we express God's love to the world. Looking at the chart below can help you to begin exploring whether singleness is a way of life that fits in with your nature.

ARE YOU CALLED TO SINGLENESS?

The call to singleness builds on a combination of human traits and a special gift of God's grace that creates a special affinity to "the foundational style of life in which this vocation has to be realized," according to Dr. Adrian Van Kamm.* Consider whether you exhibit the traits, attitudes, and preferences below:

Trait or Preference	Usually	Sometimes	Rarely	Not at all
You are invigorated by singleness and welcome it.				
You are aware that there is a substantial difference between how you feel about being single and how those feel who find it an unwelcome experience.				

*In his introduction to Susan Muto's book *Celebrating Singleness* (Image, 1985). This list is drawn from several books that discuss singleness and from conversations with single adults, not from Dr. Van Kamm's ideas exclusively.

Trait or Preference	Usually	Sometimes	Rarely	Not at all
You experience a feeling of special closeness with God in times of solitude.				
You enjoy the freedom of being able to choose to be in ministry in ways that married persons are not as free to choose (short-term mission work, special outreaches of the church, retreats, etc.).				
You have dealt with issues of your sexuality and have clear direction about how you are to honor God in this area of your life.				
You have the ability to set limited and realistic goals for personal and spiritual development.				
You can set limits on relationships and do not let others make special demands on you (at work, in the church, in your family, in friendships) because they assume you can do more than marrieds.				
You have a sense of fulfillment about your job and find it a place of ministry.				
You find increasing peace, joy, and intimacy with God.				
You look at the future as filled with possibilities for you as a single person.				
You enjoy intimate relationships with family members and friends that satisfy your emotional needs and make you feel that life is fulfilling.				

If your responses to many of the questions is "almost always" or "frequently," you might want to talk with a spiritual friend, write in your journal, or spend time in prayer to discern whether God may be calling to you in this exercise. Perhaps the single life offers possibilities for "unhindered devotion" that you should consider. Approaching life with a sense of ministry can transform our daily activities, our work, and our encounters with others. When we see our situation as God's call, we can be happily and enthusiastically single. A strong sense of self, a clear of identity that comes from knowing the gifts God has given us and how we can use them, contributes to emotional and spiritual stability.

A call to singleness is not, however, a call to weirdness. It is not permission to be asocial or anti-social, to never bathe or to give up working on table manners and interpersonal skills. It is also not a call to isolation, to living like a hermit. Single or married, we all need love, support, and community. These needs don't disappear because we are called to singleness. Single people may have to be more deliberate than married people in seeing that these needs are met, especially if they live alone or far from family. A community of faith can offer a loving environment for this. A Sunday school class or singles group can challenge us in our spiritual growth, support us in times of need, and draw us into ministry to our community and the world. Having a regular prayer partner or spiritual friend or being part of a discipleship or accountability group is also valuable. This is true in anyone's spiritual life to help in processing feelings and experiences, but it can be especially important for those who are single.

Being single does not mean withdrawing from relationships. Relationships with others are one of the most challenging parts of life. If we have rough places that need to be polished, interaction with others will bring that to our attention in unmistakable ways. I have often said that even I might be able to be a holy person if I lived in a hermitage and devoted all my time to prayer, contemplation, and spiritual reading. If I never had to see or interact with others, I could more easily love them and remain detached from the world. It's putting up with all the turkeys that challenges my inner peace and disturbs my focus on God. Being alone all the time would solve that problem. But very few of us are called to live the life of a hermit. God calls most of us to live out our holiness in the midst of ordinary, daily life.

Even though I am clear about my desire to continue living as a single, however, other people don't always understand. People who care about us and want the best for us may believe that "the best" includes marriage. Some people cannot conceive of others being happy while not married, even if our lives seem full. They may even think that we fill our lives with busyness in order not to feel lonely or to be alone (and I did that early on in my singleness to avoid looking inward). One day a few years ago my daughter asked me, "Mom, are you happy?"

"Yes, honey, I'm very happy."

"But I mean, do you like your life?"

"Yes, I like my life. I like it a lot. I like it better right now than maybe I ever have. Why do you ask?"

"Well, it looks boring to me. And I want you to be happy."

"I am happy, and for me my life is not boring. I love you. I love Casey (the man I've dated for years). I love my job. I love my house and my car and my dog. I have a good life, and I'm grateful for it."

"Okay, but it still looks boring to me!"

Substitute "sad" or "lonely" or "unfulfilled" for "boring," and you'd have what many seem to think is the lot of the single adult. But I am not any of those things, in spite of what my daughter or others might think. This does not mean that I am always deliriously happy about my life or that I never feel alone—but married people are not always deliriously happy, and the aloneness of being in a bad marriage and trying to hide it can be almost crushing. And married people feel lonely from time to time even in good marriages. Being alone is part of being human. A modern novel that I read (I think it was *Man's Fate* by Andre Malraux) said that every one of us is serving a life sentence in solitary confinement. That author was writing about the aloneness that is a part of being an individual. In that way of thinking, we are all alone. We exist as individual human beings, and none of us can be completely known by or completely know another person. We enter life and leave it accompanied only by God, whether we marry or not, whether we live with a family or not. But the good news is that God is always with us. No circumstance of life can take that from us, and in relationship with God we find our lasting wholeness and our home. I feel comfortable with being single. I experience God's love for me and God's presence in my life.

Once we become identified as a confirmed single, there are other challenges. Some people have the attitude that single adults ought to do things that need to be done because we don't have a spouse or children to care for. People may assume that the single son or daughter will care for the aging parent, that the single aunt or uncle will be the babysitter, that the single employee will take the long shift or work the extra hours because we have more free time and don't have a family to care for. It can be difficult to resist these pressures. But in reality, single people may have less free time than others. We have no one with whom to divide the daily tasks of running a household. There is only one person to take care of the car maintenance, to do the upkeep on the house, to balance the checkbook and pay the bills, to take care of the lawn, to clean the house and do the laundry and shopping. Single people can't split up those tasks with a spouse. A part of being happily single is learning how not to let others take advantage of us. In fact, we have to make a commitment to ourselves to care for ourselves. The absence of a spouse or children means that we are the ones who have to set the limits. We must determine how much we will work, how many hours we can volunteer at church or in the community and still be healthy. It is easy to fall into a pattern of working late, not eating wisely, and not exercising when there is no one waiting at home to comment. Single people face special challenges in these areas. One test of whether we are called to single life is facing these challenges and being invigorated by them.

You may not know whether you are called to be single. It took me years to decide that this way of living fits with who I am. But all of us can commit to an on-going appraisal of our call. If you are single today, as I am, for today at least we know that we are called to serve God as singles. Wherever we are on any given day, in that time and place we are meant to serve God. Ultimately, God's call may take us onward to another situation, but for today we serve where we are, as we are.

---

[1]Tal Ilan, *Jewish Women in Greco-Roman Palestine: An Inquiry into Image and Status* (Hendrickson Publishers, Inc. 1996), 63.

[2]Susan Annette Muto, *Celebrating the Single Life: A Spirituality for Single Persons in Today's World* (New York: Doubleday, 1982), 56.

[3]Jack Hayford, *The Beauty of Spiritual Language: A Journey Toward the Heart of God*. Quoted in *Homiletics*, September 1997, 62.

CHAPTER 14

"IF THERE'S ANYTHING
I CAN DO..."

People continually say to those in crisis, "If there's anything I can do, you just call me." We make those offers with good intentions; we want to do something. We feel helpless in the face of others' pain, and doing something takes away some of that sense of helplessness. Think of all the casseroles and cakes church members bring to those who have had a death in the family. We care. When people in pain go uncomforted, it is not because of lack of caring.

But often when we make the offer "If there's ever anything I can do ..." we make it because we can't think of anything to do. We frequently say things like this to people going through divorce or other loss. And then, being unable to "fix" whatever is wrong, we retreat from the one who is in pain. I have been guilty of this many times.

The Bible story of the healing of Bartimaeus (Mark 10:46-52) has taught me some important lessons about how we can help those in need. Bartimaeus was a blind man who lived in Jericho. When Jesus and the disciples came to Jericho, a large crowd was waiting for them, and Bartimaeus was in the crowd. When he heard that Jesus was there, he began calling out, "Jesus, Son of David, have mercy on me!" Others in the crowd "sternly ordered him to be quiet." They didn't want Bartimaeus to disturb the important rabbi. Bartimaeus was just a blind man, after all, and probably a beggar. They didn't want this desperate person to make a scene. Can you imagine how your congregation would react if a blind person stood up during the sermon and began calling out to the preacher, "Servant of God, have mercy on me! Heal me!" If that happened in my church, ushers would probably come and escort that person away. Quickly. Such behavior isn't "appropriate" in church.

But Bartimaeus didn't call out to Jesus during a sermon. It was a crowd scene. There was probably plenty of hubbub. Other people were making noise too—but this man was calling out because he was in need. In Tennessee we're comfortable with people yelling at football games, but someone yelling in distress makes us uncomfortable. Like the people around Bartimaeus were uncomfortable. They were uncomfortable with his neediness and his desperation. They remind me of my friend Willie's saying about how we try to hide our imperfections and our pain by "dressing up pretty for Jesus." Like those in the crowd who wanted Bartimaeus to be quiet, we don't want our neediness or the neediness of others to be too obvious. We want everyone to seem happy, to wear nice clothes, even to pretend that nothing is wrong in their lives. In most church settings, we put on a happy face, "dress up pretty for Jesus," and try to set our problems aside.

That's not the way life is, of course, but a picture of our average congregation on Sunday morning would belie that truth. Neediness is so untidy. Desperation is so unsettling. Bartimaeus's townspeople might have been ashamed of him and his blindness because they considered it a sign of God's judgment. (There's another story of Jesus and the disciples encountering a blind man. In this instance the disciples asked Jesus, "Rabbi, who sinned, this man or his parents, that he was born blind?" (John 9:2). In the disciples' way of thinking, that man's blindness had to have been caused by someone's sin.) Bartimaeus's condition might reflect badly on them and their town. Whatever their reasons, the people in the crowd wanted Bartimaeus to be quiet and not draw attention to himself.

In a similar way, we often want people who are in pain to be quiet and invisible. We're much too well brought up to say so outright, of course. We want to hang on to the illusion that people in our congregation don't have "those kinds of problems"—domestic violence or infidelity or drug abuse or alcoholism or sexual abuse or whatever we think doesn't fit with our image. We don't want to get a bad reputation in the community—"that church that has all the alcoholics" or "that church that has all the poor people." We're not "that kind" of people.

Sometimes we want people to keep quiet because their loss and tragedy are unsettling to us. They remind us of our own fragility, our vulnerability. I recently attended a memorial service for a young woman I have known since she was a child. She died of cancer at age twenty-five. During the last weeks of her life, I could hardly talk about her illness without crying. I loved her and love her family, but there was more going on for me than her illness and death. I finally realized that her illness was opening the door to one of my deep fears, that of losing my own daughter. Emily has been seriously ill a few times in her life, and the possibility that she could die evokes in me a depth of terror that I cannot begin to articulate. My difficulty with this other young woman's illness and death came from what was going on inside me.

When my younger sister died many years ago, I saw my mother stagger under the burden of her grief. It became clear to me as the years passed that a parent never completely "recovers" from the death of a child; there is always a void, a sense of incompleteness about life. For the rest of Mother's life, when she talked about my sister there was ineffable sorrow in her face. In my adulthood, my brother and his wife have lost two children to death. For me, the possibility that a child can die is very real. It is not a remote possibility. And praying for my friends as their daughter's illness worsened kept forcing me to acknowledge that possibility. When we are deeply troubled by another person's pain, it may be because of emotions or fears we don't want to deal with. Confronting others' pain may cause us to consider that the same could happen to us, and so we prefer that they keep quiet. Pain that we have buried, that we may even be unaware of consciously, can emerge when we are close to those in pain, causing us to feel uneasy with them.

We may also turn away from those in pain because we cannot fix what is wrong. We don't know what to say, and so we don't visit or call. The way that Jesus dealt with Bartimaeus shows me that there is always something that we can do to help—but it does not hinge on fixing the problem.

The first thing that Jesus did was to stop and notice Bartimaeus. Taking time to stop, to let those in need know that we care, is important. We all need someone to notice us. No special skills are required. Taking time to put aside what we are doing and give someone our full attention, even for a few moments, is an affirmation that they matter to us. This sounds easy, but I find it difficult. When I'm working at the computer and the phone rings, my tendency is to try to keep on working while I take the call. If I'm in the middle of a task and someone comes into my office, though I talk with the visitor, my eyes and my mind often stray back to the papers on my desk. I even find my hand creeping back toward the pen so I can make notes on what I am thinking while I pretend to pay attention to the person in front of me. It takes self-discipline to focus on the one person before us, or even on one person at a time in a group. Our lives are filled with many demands, and it is easy to fall into the pattern of not giving anyone our full attention. But this focus on individuals is a trait that we see over and over in Jesus. He was never too busy to take time for the solitary person. The woman with the issue of blood touched him while he was on the way to heal Jairus's daughter, and he stopped and turned to her (Luke 8:41-48). Zaccheus was up in a tree, and Jesus stopped a procession to talk with him (Luke 19:1-5). Martha interrupted Jesus as he spoke with Mary, and Jesus turned to her (Luke 10:38-42).

When Jesus came through Jericho he was on his way to Jerusalem, where he would face the most important struggle of his life. But he still took time to turn to Bartimaeus. Jesus reminds us in this story that each person we encounter is worthy of our full attention. When we give it, we are saying that they matter. When we don't give it, we say by our actions that whatever else we are doing is more important than they are. Though going to Jerusalem was part of Jesus' mission, so was stopping to turn to Bartimaeus. In the same way, whatever our life's mission is, the people we encounter along the way are part of it. Paying attention to them is an important part of our journey.

The next thing Jesus does in his encounter with Bartimaeus is remarkable. Jesus asks him, "What do you want me to do for you?" Here is a blind man calling out for mercy, and Jesus asks, "What do you want me to do for you?" Most of us would probably think the answer to that question is self-evident. But Jesus, the Messiah and the Son of God, does not assume that he knows what Bartimaeus wants and needs. That is astounding to me. The man is blind, but Jesus doesn't say anything about the blindness. Instead, he asks Bartimaeus what he wants.

If we look closely at what Jesus did here, we see the key to helping those in need: we open a door for them to name their need, to talk about it. We don't rush in and start doing things. We meet people on their terms. Thinking about how Jesus dealt with Bartimaeus has helped me to see how presumptuous it is for me to assume I know what other people need or want. Jesus respected Bartimaeus and let Bartimaeus say what they would talk about. No matter what may seem to be obviously awry in someone's life, we cannot assume that what we see is their greatest need. We cannot know another's deep needs. Even if we see specific needs, we can begin only by inviting others into conversation. We stay with them, and we listen. They set the boundaries; they determine what they want us to know. We show them that we care, and eventually they may talk about their deep needs, their losses, and their dreams. It is a privilege to be with others as they talk honestly about their pain and their hopes.

Several years ago I was on a late-night flight from Philadelphia on an almost empty plane. There were probably no more than thirty people on board, scattered among many rows with six seats across. During take-off, I looked to my left to see the lights of the city as the plane banked. When I did, I noticed a young man about twenty-five or so sitting by the window across the aisle and one row back. He was crying, silently. Tears were washing down his cheeks. From time to time he would swipe the back of his hand across his face, moving the tears out of the way. There was no one else seated in my row or in his. I sat praying for him, but it did not seem that praying was enough. After a few minutes of arguing with myself that whatever it was, was none of my business and that I should leave him alone, I got up and moved to the aisle seat beside him. I had never done anything like this before, but I decided that having noticed his pain, I could not ignore it. I said, "Look, I don't mean to intrude, and if you want me to leave, just say so and I will. But I couldn't help noticing that you are upset, and I wondered if you would like to talk about it."

He began talking. He'd just left his mother, who was dying, and he knew he would probably never see her again. He was one of several children, and neither his dad nor his siblings was able to talk about her approaching death. He was the only one. He and his mother had always been close, and they had talked openly about her death. He was glad for that, but he had been holding in the sadness while he was with her. Now he could not hold it in any longer. He talked for most of the flight. I asked an occasional question, but apart from that I said almost nothing. Before the flight landed and I got off, we exchanged business cards. A few months later, at Thanksgiving time, I got a card from him in the mail. He told me about his mother's death and funeral and thanked me for doing so much for him. I had done very little, from my perspective. I had listened, and that was really all. But that meant a great deal to him. In the years since then we have corresponded from time to time, and in some way he always refers to my great kindness. What was my great deed? I noticed him, and I listened. Anyone could do what I did.

I learned another lesson from him. I learned that my skills, knowledge, and experience are irrelevant to those in pain. His situation was one about which I could do absolutely nothing. My mother had died not long before this, and I knew I could not alleviate his grief. Because of that, I felt no need to offer advice or suggest solutions. If it had been a job situation or a relationship problem, I probably would have been tempted to begin problem-solving. I would try to fix it—and that would have interfered with my doing what he really needed. But because I recognized that I could not "fix" what was bothering him, I felt no need to try to do anything more than listen. In doing nothing except listen, I learned that it is the one thing I can always offer.

In the Bible story, Bartimaeus's answer to Jesus' question was straightforward: "Lord, that I might see again"(Mark 10:51, AP). I had read this story many times before I noticed that last word—"again." That word conveys great loss. Bartimaeus had not been born blind. At one time he had been able to see. Losing one's sight is always a tragedy, but in Jesus' day it was an even greater disaster than it is now. There was little medical help and no hope of recovering sight. Going blind probably meant loss of livelihood and that would mean loss of position in the community and loss of self-sufficiency. Bartimaeus was a man who knew about grief and loss. He probably thought that this loss had changed his life forever, until he heard about Jesus.

Healing did not begin only when Bartimaeus called out. His healing began much earlier, when someone helped him to have hope. Someone helped Bartimaeus believe that he was worth being healed. And someone—maybe the same person, maybe someone else—told him about Jesus. Jesus' turning to the blind man was the culmination of many things that God had been doing, through many people who had been part of Bartimaeus's life. Grace is at work in our lives and in the lives of others to bring us to the point that we ask God for wholeness. But when Jesus spoke to Bartimaeus and Bartimaeus answered, God touched Bartimaeus in a special way. Each time we name a need before God, we open the door for grace to intersect our lives and others' lives in response to that need. And when we hear someone name a need, we have the opportunity to become conscious co-workers in what God wants to do.

The small acts that brought Jesus and Bartimaeus together at this moment were invisible or had at least seemed random, but they were not. God uses all sorts of means to bring us to our personal "healing moment," the time when we reach out for grace and receive it in ways that change our life. God uses all sorts of people to move us to the place where we encounter the One who helps us to "see again." Along the road to healing, we need people who renew our hope and help us to believe we are worth healing. And along the way, we can be those people for others. We don't have to do big things. We don't have to have the answers for those who have suffered great loss. We only have to listen and care. We do not have the power to fix what is wrong after someone tells us what it is, anyway. Only

God can do that. But we can be, to borrow again from Henri Nouwen, "living reminders" of the God who stops, takes notice, and responds in love.

Trouble comes to all of us. Though God rejoices with us in the good times and loves to hear us laugh, hard times seem to open the door on important spiritual issues that we may not be willing to face in easier times. Our personal struggles offer us a direct experience of the grace of God; and as we walk with others through their difficulties, we experience God's grace indirectly as it flows through us to them. Because of the power of that grace, we are changed for the better. Whether we are the one in great pain or the one who stands by listening in love, God is present with us in a special way during these times. As C. S. Lewis wrote in *The Problem of Pain*, "God whispers to us in our pleasures, speaks in our conscience, but shouts in our pains."[1]

As I was working on this chapter, one of my brothers asked me if it is about divorce. I said that it was more a word of hope about how we can help those who are going through hard times, those who are struggling with life. He said, "That's pretty much everybody, isn't it?"

He's right. I have come to believe that nearly everyone carries heavy burdens. Some of the pains and burdens are obvious, and some are very well hidden. Even people who are dressed up pretty for Jesus—perhaps especially they—need the opportunity to name the pain in their hearts. They need someone who cares and who will listen. As we take time to do that, we participate in God's work of bringing wholeness. We become channels of the grace that mends broken lives and broken hearts.

---

[1] C. S. Lewis. *The Problem of Pain* (London: The Centenary Press, 1940), 81.

LOOKING DEEPER

You may want to look a little more deeply into some of the topics mentioned in this book. Here are some books that address some of the subjects. This list reflects my reading and my perspective on many of the ideas I have written about. It is arranged by chapter topics. In most cases I have indicated whether books are written from a specifically Christian perspective if that is not clear from the title.

Special Note: An asterisk (★) indicates that the book is out of print but may be available at your local library.

CHAPTER 1: BROKEN DREAMS

Blomquist, Jean. *Wrestling Till Dawn: Awakening to Life in Times of Struggle* (Nashville, Tenn.: Abingdon Press, 1997). Blomquist explores how she experienced God's grace in the struggles of a marriage ending, during chronic illness, in financial difficulties, in personal failure, and in changing family relationships. She is a good writer, and the book is both helpful and hopeful.

★Brown, Robert McAfee. *Creative Dislocation: The Movement of Grace.* (Nashville, Tenn.: Abingdon Press, 1980). I found this book personally helpful during the time immediately following my divorce. Brown traces how upheavals in his life have led him to experience God's grace in new ways. He examines bad decisions and the failure to discern God's will and shows how God used them to help him grow. It is a hopeful and encouraging book.

King, Martin Luther, Jr. "Shattered Dreams" in *Strength to Love* (Minneapolis, Minn.: Augsburg Fortress Press, 1981). This sermon explores the Apostle Paul's intimate acquaintance with planning one thing and experiencing another. Dr. King acknowledges the poignancy of realizing that cherished dreams are not going to be realized.

Monroe, Robin P. *In This Very Hour: Devotions in Your Time of Need: Loss of a Dream* (Nashville, Tenn.: Broadman & Holman,1994). This is a series of 31 short daily devotions that deal in general with loss of a dream—about children, career, or other things. An epilogue deals with the birth of new dreams.

CHAPTER 2: QUESTIONS

Norris, Kathleen. *Dakota: A Spiritual Geography* (New York: Ticknor & Fields, 1993). This book is an account of Norris's rediscovery of faith after she and her husband moved to North Dakota. A part of her journey including examining human attachment to what we wish were true in the face of reality that contradicts our illusions. This book is simultaneously about struggle and hope. Norris is honest about her questions, and the book offers an engaging and haunting picture of how inner and outer reality converge in the spiritual journey.

Peck, M. Scott. *The Road Less Traveled* (New York: Simon & Schuster Trade, 1998). This widely popular book begins with the sentence, "Life is difficult." Peck, a psychiatrist, examines how our illusions (and the desire to cling to them) keep us from enjoying life for the wonder that it is. The popularity of the book attests to its helpfulness and insights into the struggles of modern life. Though not specifically Christian, the book acknowledges the need for spirituality in a healthy life.

CHAPTER 3: DEPRESSION

Benson, Robert. *Between the Dreaming and the Coming True* (HarperSanFrancisco, 1996). Benson explores his evangelical upbringing, his spiritual journey as an adult, and his struggles with depression. He is a talented writer.

Gregg-Schroeder, Susan. *In the Shadow of God's Wings: Grace in the Midst of Depression* (Nashville, Tenn.: Upper Room Books, 1997). Gregg-Schroeder, an ordained minister, chronicles her journey into depression, her discoveries about how the past was affecting her in the present, and the gifts that walking with God through the shadows offers us. This book puts depression into the context of spiritual struggle for people of faith. Very helpful.

CHAPTER 4: FAMILY PATTERNS

Bradshaw, John. *Homecoming: Reclaiming and Championing Your Inner Child* (New York: BantamBooks, 1992). PBS series host John Bradshaw calls the discovery of the inner child the most important part of his extensive work in healing emotional and spiritual wounds. This very readable book uses many stories to explore how early wounds can limit us in every part of adult life. Bradshaw offers strategies for "reclaiming" the power, creativity, energy, and joy that can be ours when we confront and deal with the wounds of our past. Though Bradshaw is Christian, the book is not specifically so.

*Foster, Carolyn. *The Family Patterns Workbook: Breaking Free from Your Past and Creating a Life of Your Own* (New York: Tarcher/Putnam, 1993). This book comes from Foster's work with a program called "Writing from Your Roots." It is a workbook to be used privately. Major divisions include "Tracing Family Patterns," "Getting to the Roots," and "Patterning New Growth." She helps users explore family communication styles, how family shapes our sense of self, and how we can remedy the negatives and build on the positives of our family patterns.

Leman, Kevin. *The Birth Order Book: Why You Are the Way You Are* (Ada, Mich.: Fleming H. Revell, 1993). This readable and entertaining book by a Christian psychologist examines how order of birth (oldest, youngest, middle child) affects relationships with parents, spouse, children, and God, and how it influences choices of mates and relationships within blended families.

CHAPTER 5: LEARNING TO TRUST GOD

King, Martin Luther, Jr. "Our God Is Able" and "Antidotes for Fear" in *Strength to Love* (Minneapolis, Minn.: Augsburg Fortress, 1981). These two sermons remind us to face squarely our fears and discover how God will act in our lives when we do.

CHAPTER 6: FORGIVENESS

Donnelly, Doris. *Learning to Forgive* (Nashville, Tenn.: Abingdon Press, 1986). We hurt those we love and are hurt by them and others. Dr. Donnelly shows how learning to forgive is key to sustaining relationships. The book deals with the reasons for and consequences of unforgiveness and offers models for moving toward forgiveness. Specifically Christian, readable, and helpful.

CHAPTER 7: SINGLES IN THE CHURCH

Collier-Slone, Kay. *Single in the Church: New Ways to Minister with 52 Percent of God's People* (Bethesda, Md.: Alban Institute, 1992). Active in singles ministry in the Episcopal Church, Dr. Collier-Slone in this book describes forms of successful singles programs. A special feature of the book is litanies or liturgies for special times in the lives of singles, such as a service of blessing for someone newly single on entering this new lifestyle.

★Efird, James M. *Marriage and Divorce: What the Bible Says* (Nashville, Tenn.: Abingdon Press, 1985). This book examines Old Testament and New Testament scriptures that refer to divorce. It's a thorough look at what the Bible has to say. Efird is compassionate in dealing with the issues of divorce, while dealing carefully with the scriptures.

Koons, Carolyn A. and Michael J. Anthony. *Single Adult Passages: Uncharted Territories* (Grand Rapids, Mich.: Baker Books, 1995). This book reports the results of Koons and Anthony's survey of hundreds of singles in the church on many aspects of singleness. If you want to see how you compare in attitudes, income, interests, and many other ways with singles in the church, this book will tell you. It also has sections on the history of singles in the church and suggestions about the church and singles in the future.

CHAPTER 8: SELF-IMAGE AND SELF-LOVE

Dowling, Colette. *The Cinderella Complex: Woman's Hidden Fear of Independence* (New York: Pocket Books, 1990). Any female who has read a fairy tale and wished for Prince Charming in her life can learn from this book. It explores how learned helplessness and dependence hold women back from living their lives fully. Not specifically Christian.

Erdman, Cheri K. *Nothing to Lose: A Guide to Sane Living in a Larger Body* (San Francisco: HarperSanFrancisco, 1995). After years of roller-coaster dieting, psychotherapist Dr. Erdman realized that she had been putting off being happy and fulfilled until she was thin. She set out to find a way of accepting herself as she was. This book looks at the myths and realities associated with "ideal" weight, at self-concept and self-image, and at how larger women can live sanely in a culture obsessed with thinness. The book includes an appendix for therapists and one for those interested in starting a support group to discuss the ideas of the book. Not specifically Christian.

Higgs, Liz Curtis. *One Size Fits All and Other Fables* (Nashville, Tenn.: Thomas Nelson, 1993). In a funny and insightful way, this book traces one woman's journey from self-recrimination for being fat to self-acceptance. A fervent evangelical Christian, Higgs struggled for years with fatness/thinness as an issue of discipleship and often found the church less than helpful. Higgs shows how for her dealing with old wounds was a prerequisite for self-acceptance of her body.

Jones, James W. *In the Middle of This Road We Call Our Life: The Courage to Search for Something More* (San Francisco: HarperSanFrancisco, 1996). This book by psychologist Jones describes the struggle to distinguish between the false selves we adopt and our true self. Jones believes that our true self, fulfilling relationships, and fullness of life can be found only in recognizing and attending to our deep spiritual yearnings. A series of case histories makes the book entertaining and readable. Not specifically Christian.

Peck, M. Scott. *Further Along the Road Less Traveled: The Unending Journey toward Spiritual Growth* (New York: Simon and Schuster Trade, 1998). In this book Peck extends the ideas presented in *The Road Less Traveled*. The book's twelve chapters are divided into sections titled "Growing Up," "Knowing Your Self," and "In Search of a Personal God." He addresses the cultural acknowledgment of the human need for meaning beyond materialism and self-expression. Not specifically Christian.

CHAPTER 10: IDENTITY IN CHRIST

Broyles, Anne. *Journaling: A Spirit Journey* (Nashville, Tenn.: Upper Room Books, 1988). Broyles explores the role of journaling in Christian growth. She examines six aproaches to journaling, including journaling from scripture and from daily life. Each of the six descriptions of journaling includes exercises to explore the approach. This book is a helpful introduction to the spiritual discipline of journaling.

Edwards, Tilden H. *Spiritual Friend: Reclaiming the Gift of Spiritual Direction* (Mahway, NJ: Paulist, 1997). This book is a classic on the subject of spiritual direction. Edwards works with the Shalem Institute outside Washington, D.C., to train spiritual directors. The book deals with our culture's lack of acceptance of spiritual ways of knowing. It defines what a spiritual friend is and gives guidance in how to find and to be one. There is also a chapter on group spiritual direction.

Johnson, Ben Campbell. *Calming the Restless Spirit: A Journey toward God* (Nashville, Tenn.: Upper Room Books, 1997). This is a book for "seekers," those who yearn for a relationship with God and are not quite sure how to proceed. It is aimed at those who have questions about organized religion and are beginners in spiritual practices. The tone is welcoming and reassuring. I would give this book to people who want "something more" in their lives but are resistant to religious structures and language.

Landgraf, John R. *Singling: A New Way to Live the Single Life* (Louisville, Ky.: Westminster John Knox Press, 1990). This is a good book on seeking wholeness as a person, regardless of whether one is married or not. It deals helpfully with ethical questions related to sexuality and sexual expression. Though written from a Christian foundation by a Christian theologian, the book is not dogmatic.

Mulholland, M. Robert, Jr. *Shaped by the Word: The Power of Scripture in Spiritual Formation* (Nashville, Tenn.: Upper Room Books, 1985). Reading and studying the Bible is foundational to Christian growth. Mulholland introduces a way of approaching Bible reading to be formed into the image of Christ (in contrast to traditional ways of reading for information). This is a helpful book that can set readers free of ought-tos about Bible reading and Bible study and help them find a way of reading the Bible that deepens prayer life.

Smith, Hannah Whitall. *The Christian's Secret of a Happy Life* (Ada, Mich.: Fleming H. Revell, 1991). This is a classic on how to find peace and happiness through discerning and doing the will of God. It looks at obstacles to living by faith and talks in practical and straightforward terms about issues such as being swayed by our emotions and finding our way back to God after failure. The language is a little stilted, but the sound advice the book offers makes it worth reading.

CHAPTER 11: MEN AND WOMEN IN RELATIONSHIPS

Cloud, Henry and John Townsend. *Safe People: How to Find Relationships That Are Good for You and Avoid Those That Aren't* (Grand Rapids, Mich.: Zondervan, 1995). Written by Christian psychologists/counselors, this book helps readers consider how to find friendships and romantic relationships that will move them toward being the people God wants them to be. Divided into three sections—description of "unsafe" people, helps for readers to assess whether/ why they attract such people, and descriptions of safe people—the book aims to help readers find sustainable, healthy relationships with persons they can trust.

Gray, John. *Men Are from Mars, Women Are from Venus: A Practical Guide for Improving Communication & Getting What You Want in Your Relationships* and *Mars and Venus on a Date* (New York: HarperCollins, 1993, and HarperCollins, 1997). The best seller *Men Are from Mars, Women Are From Venus* discusses in entertaining ways the differences between the ways most men and most women communicate. *Mars and Venus on a Date* explores what Dr. Gray calls the "five stages of dating" and tells how to find lasting and fulfilling relationships. Both books encourage self-examination and understanding of those who see the world differently. Gray oversimplifies what men and women are like and need, but the books offer some helpful insights. Not specifically Christian. First title also available in Spanish: *Los Homres Son de Marte, Las Mujeres Son de Venus* (HarperCollins, 1995).

Jones, Ann R. and Susan Schechter. *When Love Goes Wrong: What to Do When You Can't Do Anything Right* (New York: HarperCollins, 1993). This book about abusive partners discusses how some people control partners through verbal and emotional abuse. If you have ever felt that you are worthless and lucky to have even a bad partner, this book has something to help you. Not specifically Christian.

Pintar, Judith. *The Halved Soul: Retelling the Myths of Romantic Love* (London: Pandora, 1992). Pintar takes on the notion of finding a soul-mate (which dates back to Plato and which John Gray purports to help us do) and shows how the mysterious attractions between men and women often grow from childhood wounds rather than inherent incompleteness. She examines the stories of Eve, Lilith, Iseult, and Guenevere and explores how healthy relationships are "based on the union of two independent, healthy individuals" rather than on healing our incompleteness by finding our perfect complement. Not specifically Christian.

Tannen, Deborah. *You Just Don't Understand: Women and Men in Conversation* (New York: Ballantine Books, 1991). Tannen explores the differing conversational styles of men and women and shows how human interactions are either attempts to connect with others (intimacy) or to establish position (dependence/independence). Her work is based on extensive research in socio-linguistics and reflects careful thought about relationships. Not specifically Christian.

CHAPTER 12: SEXUALITY

*Brown, Gabrielle. *The New Celibacy: A Journey to Love, Intimacy, and Good Health in a New Age* (New York: McGraw-Hill, 1989). This book looks at the history of celibacy for both religious and secular reasons and goes on to examine how modern men and women are choosing to abstain from sexual expression. It takes a somewhat spiritual (but not Christian) attitude toward reasons for and benefits of celibacy and examines strategies for minimizing sexual arousal. Dr. Brown takes a clinical rather than popular approach to the subject.

Nelson, James B. *Body Theology* (Louisville, Ky.: Westminster John Knox Press, 1992). Hailed as a ground-breaking book when published, *Body Theology* aims to help readers rediscover the tie between sexuality and spirituality. Specifically, it deals with the male body and male sexuality as a means for exploring incarnational theology. It looks at issues of aging, homosexuality, and biomedical questions. It is specifically Christian and highly regarded in many circles, but it is not an easy read.

CHAPTER 13: THE CALL TO SINGLENESS

Cloud, Henry and John Townsend. *Boundaries: When to Say Yes; When to Say No to Take Control of Your Life* (Grand Rapids, Mich.: Zondervan, 1992). In this book Christian psychologists Cloud and Townsend look at developing a clear sense of self in order not to allow others to impose on us and direct our lives. They deal with learning to say no, finding personal maturity and autonomy (including some helpful adult-children-and-their-parents case histories), and establishing healthy patterns in work and social relationships. There is an accompanying video series for group use with leader's guide available. Though written from a conservative/evangelical framework, the book gives helpful advice and raises good questions about relationships.

*Harayda, Janice. *The Joy of Being Single: Stop Putting Your Life on Hold and Start Living!* (New York: Doubleday, 1986). This is an easy-to-read and entertaining book. It begins with a quiz to help the reader assess whether she or he has put life on hold or is living fully. Harayda discusses issues such as making a house into a home, building friendships, and not becoming married to a job or career. Not specifically Christian, though faith is mentioned as a part of living happily single.

Job, Rueben, comp. *A Guide to Spiritual Discernment* (Nashville, Tenn.: Upper Room Books, 1996). This book offers a forty-day journey in discerning the will of God. Its format includes a structure for a daily time of prayer, scripture and spiritual reading, and reflection, with selections keyed to subjects such as discerning God's will in a broken world or in a broken body. It can be used by a group or by an individual.

Miller, Wendy. *Learning to Listen: A Guide for Spiritual Friends* (Nashville, Tenn.: Upper Room Books, 1993). This book offers a definition of spiritual friendship as a deliberate relationship of mutual support in spiritual growth. It offers guidance for finding and being a spiritual friend and establishing personal spiritual disciplines, as well as a pattern for using the Gospel of Matthew for meditative reading and personal journaling. This is much more readable (and shorter) than many of the almost-classics on the subject of spiritual friendship.

Smith, Harold Ivan. *Holy! Me? The Single Adult's Guide to the Spiritual Journey* (Nashville, Tenn.: Abingdon Press, 1997). Smith has written numerous books for and about singles. This one has five sections, one an overview of the spiritual life for singles, followed by sections on scripture and spiritual reading, praying, journaling, and making space in your life for spiritual pursuits. Its workbook format includes six "icons"(as on a computer screen) to guide users through the activities. Smith is honest, and the exploratory tone of the book is welcoming.

Clements, Marcelle. *The Improvised Woman* (New York: Norton, 1998). Based on interviews with 100 single women, this book explores the joys and contradictions of being single and female in this time. Definitely not Christian, but honest. Includes witty essays.

CHAPTER 14: HELPING THOSE WHO HURT

Nouwen, Henri J. M. *The Wounded Healer: Ministry in Contemporary Society* (New York: Doubleday, 1972; Image version, 1990). The cover of this book carries the statement that is its central message: "In our own woundedness, we can become a source of life for others." Nouwen explores how our scars, pain, and incompleteness can equip us to help others experience God's grace and healing.

Nouwen, Henri J. M. *The Living Reminder* (San Francisco: HarperSanFrancisco, 1984). This book aims to help all who follow Christ to understand how we can be reminders of Christ by both our presence and our absence in the lives of those we encounter. Nouwen writes simply, clearly, and powerfully—here and in all his books.

ABOUT THE AUTHOR

MARY LOU REDDING serves as the managing editor of *The Upper Room* daily devotional guide. She has worked as a magazine feature writer, taught college-level composition, and leads retreats and writers' workshops. Her writings have appeared in numerous magazines including *Alive Now, Weavings, The Christian Communicator,* and *Pockets.* She contributed to the book *Writing to Inspire* and is winner of a writing award from the National Educational Press Association for one of her children's stories.

Mary Lou is a former president of the Associated Church Press, an organization of almost 200 religious periodicals in the United States and Canada. She serves on the board of *Horizons Magazine,* the magazine published by Presbyterian women for the Presbyterian Church (USA). She has a Bachelor of Arts degree in English Literature and a Master of Arts in Rhetoric and Writing. The author has also completed further study at Vanderbilt Divinity School.

Her hobbies include sewing, cooking, playing racquetball, and reading in spirituality and psychology. She was founding chair of the Single Adult Council of the Tennessee Annual Conference of the United Methodist Church and is active in the single adult ministry of Brentwood United Methodist Church in Brentwood, Tennessee.